The Blitz

Bombers over Britain 1940–41

Books

Front cover: St Paul's Cathedral stands defiant on London's skyline during the Blitz. (Colourisation by colourbyrjm)

Title page: Members of the Pioneer Corps taking a break from clearance work in the Guildhall, London, on 12 March 1941. (Historic Military Press)

Acknowledgements

The editorial team would like to thank Robert Mitchell for his assistance with the images in this publication.

Published by Key Books

An imprint of Key Publishing Ltd

PO Box 100

Stamford

Lincs PE19 1XQ

www.keypublishing.com

Original edition published as *The Blitz: Bombers Over Britain 1940-1941* by Key Publishing Ltd © 2020

ISBN 978 1 80282 209 0

Typeset by SJmagic DESIGN SERVICES, India.

Contents

Overleaf: One of the many buildings badly damaged in the raid on London on 10 May 1941 was St Mary-le-Bow Church in Cheapside. In the subsequent fire, the church's bells crashed to the ground. **(Historic Military Press)**

Introduction

For months, the Spitfires and Hurricanes of the RAF's Fighter Command had held the Germans at bay. Day after day and night after night, in Winston Churchill's never-to-be-forgotten words, 'The Few' had defended Britain against the might of Göring's Luftwaffe. Then, on 7 September 1940 – 'Black Saturday' – everything changed. Instead of the duel in the skies between aerial warriors, the target of the German bombers became London and its people. The Blitz had begun.

For 56 out of the following 57 days and nights, London was systematically attacked in what was one of the most sustained aerial bombing campaigns in history. Worse was still to come, as the Luftwaffe's attacks soon spread to other cities around the country, including Liverpool, Bristol, Cardiff, Hull, Glasgow, Birmingham, and Belfast, among others. The bombing of Coventry in November 1940 was so severe that Nazi propagandists even coined a new word – 'Coventrieren', meaning to devastate or raze a city to the ground.

Residents in a bombed street in London during the Blitz in 1940. (Library of Congress)

The onslaught on Britain's towns and cities meant that its citizens found themselves quite literally on the front line. The outstanding heroics shown by many led to the introduction of the George Cross, which ranks alongside the Victoria Cross as the highest of civilian gallantry awards. There was, however, a darker side to those desperate eight months of the Blitz – the looting of some houses and shops, even by members of the emergency services.

By May 1941, the effectiveness of the anti-aircraft barrage and the night fighters helped put an end to the Blitz, which, Marshal of the Royal Air Force Sir Sholto Douglas later declared, had failed to achieve any strategic purpose. 'In eight months of intensive night raiding', he wrote, 'the German bomber force did not succeed in breaking the spirit of the British people or preventing the expansion of our means of production and supply'.

This is the story of the Blitz in 1940 and 1941. It was a period in which the people of Britain demonstrated that resolve of which Churchill so moving spoke: 'The lights went out and the bombs came down. But every man, woman and child in the country had no thought of quitting the struggle.'

John Grehan
2020

Fireguards on the roof of a London building demonstrate extinguishing an incendiary bomb. (Historic Military Press)

Chapter 1

Britain's Finest Hour

Britain was poised on the brink of disaster. Its army had been driven from the Continent, almost 500 fighter aircraft and their invaluable pilots had been lost over France and the Low Countries, and Hitler's forces stood victorious along the Channel coast.

Winston Churchill, after telling the British people in May 1940, following his elevation to Prime Minister, that he had nothing to offer them but blood, toil, tears and sweat, warned them on 18 June of the peril they faced following France's capitulation two days earlier:

> What General Weygand has called the Battle of France is over... the Battle of Britain is about to begin… Upon this battle depends the survival of Christian civilisation. Upon it depends our own British life, and the long continuity of our institutions and our Empire. The whole fury and might of the enemy must very soon be turned on us. Hitler knows that he will have to break us in this island or lose the war… Let us therefore brace ourselves to our duties, and so bear ourselves, that if the British Empire and its Commonwealth last for a thousand years, men will still say, 'This was their finest hour'.

Heeding Churchill's warning, across the country people stood ready for that fury to be unleashed upon them, expecting and preparing to face a German invasion. But no such invasion could be contemplated by the Germans without aerial supremacy over the English Channel and the South Coast. While, in reality, the war in the air over the Channel had never ceased, the official start of the Battle of Britain was declared to have been on 10 July 1940, a date that saw heavy attacks on British shipping, though the struggle for control over Britain's skies grew in intensity on 13 August.

Reichsmarschall Hermann Göring, Supreme Commander of the Luftwaffe, declared 13 August to be 'Adler Tag' – Eagle Day – the first day of *Unternehmen Adlerangriff* (Operation *Eagle Attack*). The Luftwaffe's objective was to destroy the RAF's ability to resist by smashing its aircraft and its airfields in a massive, unstoppable onslaught. What the Luftwaffe's planners did not fully appreciate was that Air Chief Marshal Hugh Dowding's Fighter Command had developed a sophisticated defence network, and the squadrons of Spitfires, Hurricanes, Blenheims and Defiants were ready and waiting.

This network was built upon a chain of radar stations situated around most of the south and east coasts of the country. Known as 'Chain Home', its operators could detect enemy aircraft forming up in France or over the Channel, giving the pilots of Fighter Command time to 'scramble' and be in the sky, and hopefully at altitude, in time to intercept the incoming enemy formations.

Despite the bold announcement of the start of *Eagle Attack*, the first day began badly. The weather forecast the Luftwaffe had been given had proven to be incorrect, and instead of the expected favourable conditions, there was light cloud over the Channel and a halt was called on the early operations. However, this decision was not relayed to all the airfields in time to stop the departure of large elements of the German bomber force, which continued towards England – but without its protective fighters, which remained grounded.

The Chain Home radar operators had spotted the German bombers, the largest body of which totalled some 250 aircraft in four waves, that were headed for Portsmouth. There they were met and engaged by squadrons from 10 and 11 groups. Meanwhile, 150 aircraft flew towards targets in Kent, with 87 Stukas bombing RAF Detling near Maidstone, destroying the operations block and most of the hangars. Nearly 70 airmen were killed in the raid, many of whom had been in the station mess hall at the time. Detling, though, was not a front-line station, being used as a Coastal Command airfield for look-out and observation patrols.

The Stukas returned across the Channel without being intercepted by British fighters, but others were not so fortunate. As the later waves of German bombers flew over southern England, the skies suddenly cleared, and the attackers found themselves flying in brilliant sunshine.

As the threat of a German invasion grows, British troops are pictured erecting barricades in a road in southern England during the late spring of 1940. (Historic Military Press)

Above left: An early Battle of Britain casualty. This Heinkel He 111P of Stab.KG 55, which was coded G1+FA, crashed near the Horse and Jockey Inn at Hipley, Hampshire, at 16.30 hours on 12 July 1940. (via Historic Military Press)

Above right: The fuselage of a Junkers Ju 87B of 4/StG 77, coded S2+LM, after it was shot down and crashed at St Lawrence, near Ventnor on the Isle of Wight, at 17.40 hours on 8 August 1940. (Historic Military Press)

Among the raiders was Oberleutnant Heinz Schlegel, who was flying a Dornier Do 17, which was part of a force heading for RAF Eastchurch. Before he could release any of his bombs, the Spitfires of 74 Squadron had swooped down upon his aircraft from out of the sun. 'There was rending clatter, and the starboard engine spluttered and died, the Dornier was yawning violently to the left', notes one account of the dogfight that ensued. 'A hot, yellow light flashed before Schlegel's eyes, and now the port engine was in trouble too. Breaking for cloud cover, Schlegel fought to keep the Dornier airborne, steering what he hoped was due south. Then the clouds parted, and his spirits rose exultantly, only to sink again as quickly land loomed beneath them, but it wasn't familiar terrain.'[1]

---

1. Richard Collier, *Eagle Day: Battle of Britain* (Booksales, 2003), pp.56–7.

Soldiers guard the Messerschmitt Me 109 E-1, which crashed at New Salts Farm, Shoreham-by-Sea, at 07.10 hours on 13 August 1940. This was the aircraft of Oberleutnant Paul Temme, Gruppe Adjutant of I/JG 2. (via Historic Military Press)

The Dornier crash-landed near the village of Barham in Kent. For Schlegel and his crew, the war was over.

The results on Adler Tag were very discouraging for the Germans. Though the RAF lost 24 aircraft in the air and 47 on the ground, the Luftwaffe had approximately 48 of its own aircraft shot down.

'The Sound Was Unthinkable'

The following day, 14 August, the weather limited Luftwaffe operations to spasmodic 'nuisance' attacks. Cloudy conditions continued to prevail early on 15 August but, by mid-morning, the skies had cleared and the great assault upon Fighter Command was unleashed, with 1,120 aircraft heading out across the Channel.

The radar screens of the Chain Home operators were swamped with so many echoes that they were unable to distinguish one formation from another. The massed German bombers were protected by large numbers of Messerschmitt Bf 109s and Bf 110s. The Luftwaffe's plan was to use formations of 50-plus bombers to attack airfields, radar stations and aircraft factories. The Bf 109s were to clear a path to the objectives, but not tie themselves rigidly to an escort role. The Germans reasoned that, quite apart from having to defend airfields against attack, the RAF fighters, when they scrambled to tackle the bombers, would themselves be swooped upon and destroyed by the Messerschmitts. That, at least, was the plan.

The reality proved to be quite different, with the Luftwaffe losing 76 aircraft in savage battles over southern England. Watching the drama unfold in the sky above her home in Kent was Mrs Joanna Thompson:

The sound was unthinkable, you never heard anything like it, and there, out of the sky, planes were falling blazing to the ground, parachutes with little men hanging helplessly underneath drifted towards earth, even flying boots and pieces of aircraft came down hitting the tin shelter with a terrific thud. I think it was now that this war was so close to home, that we suddenly became proud of these pilots, men and young men, who we didn't even know, yet we cheered them on in every dogfight that we saw.[2]

The day that should have seen Fighter Command irreparably crippled resulted in just 34 of its aircraft being destroyed. Göring, though, had promised Hitler that he would bring the RAF, and, by extension, the UK, to its knees, and he had no intention of giving up at this stage of the battle.

On 16 August, Stuka dive-bombers were again in action, delivering a devastating raid upon RAF Tangmere in Sussex, whilst major attacks were also undertaken by German bombers on other airfields in the south. Tangmere suffered massive damage to its installations, with many aircraft destroyed on the ground and personnel killed. But the airfield was not put out of action, and the attackers paid heavily for their efforts, with eight Stukas being shot down and a further seven damaged.

---

2. Quoted on www.battleofbritain1940.net.

Operations had been almost continuous over the previous few days, and both sides were beginning to feel the strain. Many of the German aircraft badly required maintenance, and their crews needed rest, as did the RAF pilots and ground crew who had been up each day from first light. When morning broke on 17 August to reveal empty skies, the relief was palpable. It proved to be a quiet day, but everyone knew it was just a lull before the next storm.

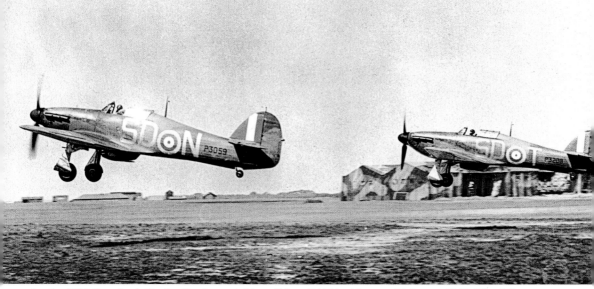

A pair of 501 Squadron's Hawker Hurricanes taking off from RAF Hawkinge on 16 August 1940. Pilot Officer Kenneth 'Hawkeye' Lee is at the controls of P3059/SD-N, whilst Pilot Officer John W Bland is flying P3028/SD-T. Bomb damage to No 5 hangar can just be seen. This was caused by the Bf 110s of Erprobungsgruppe 210 during an attack on the airfield on 12 August 1940. (Historic Military Press)

A view of Spitfires and shelters at Kenley under low-level attack by a Dornier Do 17 of KG76 on 18 August 1940. The picture was taken from the aircraft flown by Rolf von Pebal as it passed over the northern part of the airfield; the Spitfire is a 64 Squadron aircraft. This is a heavily retouched version that was used by German propaganda to present a more dramatic scene – the two largest clouds of smoke nearest the camera were, for example, not on the original. The smaller clouds beyond were, and they are probably the rest of gunfire from the Do 17 flown by Gunther Unger, as it engaged a machine gun post on the ground. (Historic Military Press)

This Junkers Ju 87 B-2 of 3/StG 2, which was coded T6+HL and had the werksnummer 5580, crashed by the B.2145 Selsey Road in West Sussex, at 13.00 hours on 16 August 1940. (Historic Military Press)

Members of the Rustington Home Guard, part of the 6th Sussex (Arundel) Battalion, pose for the camera beside a shot-down Stuka. This was a Ju 87 B-1, coded S2+JN, of 5/StG 77, which crashed at Ham Manor Golf Course, Angmering, West Sussex, at 14.23 hours on 18 August 1940. (Courtesy of Mrs Mary Taylor)

The Hardest Day

On 18 August, the Germans launched attacks in two general areas. One of these strikes was against the airfields of Kenley, Biggin Hill, Hornchurch, and North Weald, whilst the other was directed towards the Portsmouth region. While this latter raid was not small by any means, it was considered a diversionary attack, with the primary objective of the Luftwaffe being to damage the Fighter Command airfields.

This was quickly recognised by the ground controllers, who identified Kenley and Biggin Hill as being among the main targets, and fighters were pulled in from nearby airfields to help with their defence. The attack on Kenley was largely broken up, but the German bombers were able to reach Biggin Hill and release their bombs with minimal opposition; fortunately for those on the ground, most of the bombs fell short of the airfield.

Biggin Hill's satellite station, West Malling, was also hit. Retribution was swift, however, in the form of 32 and 610 squadrons. Squadron Leader Michael Crossley, leading the Hurricanes of 32 Squadron, was vectored onto the enemy. As the two formations closed over Sevenoaks, Crossley manoeuvred his squadron to meet the Germans head on. 'We sighted them as we were coming from Biggin Hill, and swung round in front of them', he later wrote. 'We didn't have to work very hard to do it. We had plenty of time to line up.'[3]

The enemy formation consisted of around 60 aircraft, which included Dornier Do 17s and Junkers Ju 88s, with an escort of 40 Bf 109s and Bf 110s. The Hurricanes tore into the German formation. Crossley continued:

Having carried out a head-on attack on the main formation of Do 215s, I climbed and saw a single 88 about 2,000ft below. I did a quarter attack on it, and after about five seconds there appeared to be an internal explosion and masses of bits flew off all around. I pulled away sharply to avoid them and flew alongside to observe the result. He jettisoned about ten small bombs and his undercarriage came down, and he glided down and crashed near Ashford.[3]

In one part of the southern, presumed diversionary attack, at around midday, 109 Stuka dive bombers, escorted by 150 Bf 109 fighters, attacked the radar station at Poling in West Sussex and the Fleet Air Arm airfield at nearby Ford. The latter suffered heavy damage, while Poling lost one of the radar towers, but the Germans paid a high price for that success, as 17 Stuka and eight Bf 109s aircraft were shot down. The Stukas were becoming obsolescent by this stage of the war, and, after such heavy losses, they played no further part in the Battle of Britain.

Though actual figures vary, both sides lost around 70 aircraft destroyed or damaged beyond repair. And so, 18 August saw the heaviest fighting to date, which has been known ever since as the 'hardest day' of the battle.

Faulty Intelligence

The loss of so many aircraft was a far more serious problem for the Germans than the British, for the country was turning out fighter planes at a far greater rate than ever before, with some 450 Spitfires and Hurricanes being added each month, compared with the 175 Bf 109s that the Germans were producing. More worrying was the loss of experienced pilots but, even in this regard, Fighter Command, while having less pilots to call upon, held a distinct advantage. This was because any British pilots who successfully baled out were quickly able to rejoin their respective squadrons, whilst any Germans who parachuted down, or force-landed, on British soil were taken prisoner.

At the start of the Battle of Britain, numbers favoured the Germans, but with the passing of every week, the odds were becoming increasingly even. But neither opponent had yet gained the upper hand, and commanders on both sides of the Channel were in earnest discussions, which resulted in Göring ordering a change of emphasis: 'We must succeed in seriously disrupting the material supplies of the enemy Air Force by the destruction of the relatively small number of aircraft engine and aluminium plants. These attacks on the enemy aircraft industry are of particular importance and should also be carried out by night'. The first of these attacks took place on the night of 19/20 August, but only on a relatively small scale.

---

3. Nick Thomas, *Hurricane Squadron Ace* (Pen & Sword, Barnsley, 2014), p.105.

Above: As seen from a Luftwaffe aircraft, bombs can be seen exploding on RAF Biggin Hill during a Luftwaffe attack in the Battle of Britain. (National Museum of Denmark)

Right: Prime Minister Winston Churchill tours a section of the South Coast to see anti-invasion defences and preparations in the summer of 1940. It is believed that this image was taken in the Dover area, circa 28 August 1940. (National Museum of Denmark)

Three Spitfire Mk.Is of 65 Squadron are pictured taking off from Hornchurch in August 1940. In the foreground is R6712, coded YT-N, and on the right R6714, coded YT-M. The latter was lost when it dived into the ground near Gateside, Fife, on 16 October 1940. (via Historic Military Press)

Meanwhile, the Luftwaffe continued its daytime raids against RAF airfields. However, German intelligence data was poor, and very often the targets were not those of primary importance in the Fighter Command defensive system.

On the night of 21/22 August, raids were undertaken across the UK from as far afield as Aberdeen and Bristol, and a heavy attack was delivered the following night when Ju 88s dropped more than 16 tons of high explosives on the aircraft works at Filton, where production was seriously disrupted. Likewise, on the night of 23/24 August, more than 200 aircraft bombed the Dunlop rubber works at Birmingham, seriously affecting tyre production.

Though variable weather conditions limited daylight raids at this stage, the tired Luftwaffe crews still continued their attacks at every opportunity. There were no grand assaults as in earlier days, for the Battle of Britain had become an attritional struggle, with each side hoping to wear down the other until the enemy was no longer capable of effective resistance.

The Few

Well aware that the result of the Battle of Britain was poised on a knife-edge, Winston Churchill stepped up to the Despatch Box in the House of Commons to deliver a speech to lift the nation's morale. 'The great air battle that has been in progress over this Island for the last few weeks has recently attained a high intensity', he warned his people. 'It is too soon to attempt to assign limits either to its scale or to its duration. We must certainly expect that greater efforts will be made by the enemy than any he has so far put forth.'

Then he delivered the good news: 'On the other hand, the conditions and course of the fighting have so far been favourable to us… At the same time the splendid – nay, astounding – increase in the output and repair of British aircraft and engines… which looks like magic, has given us overflowing reserves of every type of aircraft, and an ever-mounting stream of production both in quantity and quality'.

It was his next words that would become immortalised in the English lexicon:

The gratitude of every home in our Island, in our Empire, and indeed throughout the world, except in the abodes of the guilty, goes out to the British airmen who, undaunted by odds, unwearied in their constant challenge and mortal danger, are turning the tide of the World War by their prowess and by their devotion. Never in the field of human conflict was so much owed by so many to so few. All hearts go out to the fighter pilots, whose brilliant actions we see with our own eyes day after day.

Indeed, the duels fought in the skies were seen by the British people every day, and the growl of aero engines and the stutter of machine guns had become the soundtrack to their lives as the summer of 1940 unfolded. Mollie Mellish was a ten-year-old living in Rolvenden, near Ashford in Kent, at the time. She later recalled one day during the hop-picking school holiday:

On that day, waves of German planes came over from Dover and the Kent coast, and I remember standing in the garden looking up at so many planes that it was like a big black cloud. I tried counting the German bombers but there were too many and I had to give up. Then Spitfires and Hurricanes came on the scene, they were dogfighting with the German planes most of the day. There was lots of machine gun fire and vapour trails, maybe also the odd parachute if someone was shot down. It was a continuous loud droning noise – German and British planes had different engine noises. It was the worst day, with continuous gunfire noise. Messerschmitts were seen 'hedge-hopping' being chased back to the coast by Spitfires.[4]

On 30 August, the Germans made a tactical change that they hoped would tip the scales in their favour. Rather than having all their fighters in close support to the bombers, which restricted their flexibility, the Luftwaffe, for the first time, used a small number of Bf 109s as close escort, with a larger number flying at high altitude above.

This, however, did not deter the RAF pilots, men such as Squadron Leader Tom Gleave of 253 Squadron, when he scrambled to intercept a formation of German bombers, only to see a mass of enemy fighters above him. He did not hesitate, rushing up to meet the raiders:

He gave the first Bf 109 a four-second burst and saw his bullets hitting the engine. He saw the Perspex of the hood shatter into fragments that sparkled in the sunlight. The Bf 109 rolled onto its back, slewed, and then dropped, nose down, to the earth. Another enemy aircraft came into his sights. Gleave turned with him, firing bullets that brought black smoke from the wings before the Bf 109 dropped vertically, still smoking. Gleave narrowly missed colliding with his third victim, and then gave him a three-second burst as the Messerschmitt pulled ahead and turned into the gunfire. The cockpit seemed empty; the pilot slumped forward out of sight. The Messerschmitt fell. The German pilots were trying to maintain formation, and by now there was so much gunfire curving through the air that Gleave had the impression of flying through a gigantic golden birdcage. A fourth Messerschmitt passed slightly above Gleave, and he turned and climbed to fire into the underside of its fuselage. But after two or three seconds' firing, Gleave heard the ominous clicking that told him he had used up all his bullets. But already the fourth victim was mortally hit and rolled on its back before falling away.[5]

As August drew to a close, there seemed to be no respite for the weary combatants. The defenders were approaching untenable levels of exhaustion, with many experienced RAF pilots operating at the limits of their endurance. Relief for the hard-pressed men and machines of Fighter Command was, however, soon on hand, and its source an unlikely one – the Luftwaffe itself.

4. BBC Peoples' War website, www.bbc.co.uk/history/ww2peopleswar, Article No. A4107214.
5. Len Deighton, *Fighter* (Jonathan Cape, London, 1977), p.200.

The wreckage of a Messerschmitt Bf 109E-3 of I./JG 52 being transported on the back of a civilian lorry during September 1940. (via Historic Military Press)

Above left: This is the scene at the crash site of Hurricane V7200 of 79 Squadron, which was being flown by Sergeant Henry Albert Bolton when he crashed, while attempting a force-landing, at Halliloo Farm, Warlingham, Surrey, at the height of the Battle of Britain on 31 August 1940. Aged 21, Bolton was killed. (Historic Military Press)

Above right: A young boy sits among the wreckage of a German aircraft shot down in the Battle of Britain. Note the propeller blade behind him and the anti-landing poles in the background. (Historic Military Press)

Chapter 2

Target London

So far, since war had been declared in September 1939, the enemy's operations against the British capital and its surroundings had been generally limited in scale. Bombs had been dropped harmlessly on open ground at Addington on 8 June 1940; similarly, bombs had fallen in a field at London Colney on 26 June, killing three goats grazing there. RAF Croydon had been targeted on 15 August, whilst Kenley aerodrome's turn came three days later.

Slowly but surely, the raiders were creeping closer to the heart of London. On the night of 17 August, bombs were dropped on Woolwich and Eltham – the first to fall in the London County Council area itself.[1] On the 24th, German bombers attacked the oil tanks at Thameshaven on the Essex bank of the Thames Estuary, the blaze providing one of the first real tests for the wartime Auxiliary Fire Service (AFS).

It was not only Thameshaven that suffered during

Britain prepares for the expected onslaught. Personnel from the Auxiliary Fire Service (AFS) in the Wolverhampton area put on a demonstration for the camera. (National Museum of Denmark)

the night of 24/25 August 1940, for towns and cities across the nation were targeted, including Birmingham, Manchester, Portsmouth and Ramsgate. As a portent of what was to follow, London also received the attention of the Luftwaffe, with bombs reported to have fallen at Aldgate in the City, at Bloomsbury, Bethnal Green, Finsbury, Hackney, Stepney, Shoreditch and West Ham. 'Fires covered the whole of London's East End', noted one account, 'the night sky glowed blood red, fountains of flame bellowed out of factory windows, and wall structures came crashing down'.[2] Further out, bombs also fell at Esher, Kingston, Twickenham, Feltham and Staines.

Hitler had previously instructed that his bomber crews were not to attack the British capital without his explicit permission, which in this instance had not been granted. The attack on the City of London that night was, it would seem, unintentional – possibly a navigational error on the part of one or two bomber crews. Mistake or not, it was an act that, as we shall see, had immediate and far-reaching ramifications.

The RAF Over Berlin

Following the attacks on London and the other targets across Britain, the War Cabinet sanctioned Bomber Command's first raid on Berlin. As a result, on the night of 25/26 August, a total force of 103 aircraft, mostly Hampdens and Wellingtons, was despatched to Germany, approximately half of which attacked the capital. The results were far from inspiring:

> Berlin was found to be covered by thick cloud, which prevented accurate bombing, and a strong head wind was encountered on the return flight. The Hampdens were at the limit of their fuel capacity in such conditions, and 3 of them were lost and 3 more ditched in the sea on their return flight. The only bombs falling within the city limits of Berlin destroyed a wooden summerhouse in a garden in the suburb of

---

1. Commander Sir Aylmer Firebrace, *Fire Service Memories* (Andrew Melrose, London, 1946), p.165.
2. See www.battleofbritain1940.net.

Rosenthal and 2 people were slightly injured. The Berlin records show that many bombs fell into large farms – *Stadtgüter* – owned by the city of Berlin. The joke went round Berlin: 'Now they are trying to starve us out.'[3]

Though the British bombs were ineffectual at best, the significance of the raid was not lost on both sides, as the RAF's official historian, Denis Richards, later revealed:

Incidents of this nature were naturally galling to the Führer. It was also galling, however small the damage to industry, to have bombs falling on German cities. And it was still more galling to learn that even Berlin, 600 miles from the British bases, was not immune; for on 25/26th August… eighty-one British aircraft raided targets in the German capital. The same medicine was administered several times during the next few nights. It was not a prescription in which the Air Staff had any great confidence, as there were plenty of more important objectives much nearer; but there were political advantages to consider, which the Prime Minister was not slow to point out.[4]

Hitler Agrees

London's fate was finally sealed during a meeting between Göring and the commanders of Luftflottens II and III – Generalfeldmarschall Albert Kesselring and Generalfeldmarschall Hugo Sperrle, respectively – at The Hague on 3 September 1940. As the historian Michael Glover once wrote:

[Those present] heard a report from Luftwaffe Intelligence which claimed that 1,115 British fighters had been destroyed since 8 August, an estimate hard to reconcile with the calculation of 16 August that the RAF had only 430 fighters and a maximum production rate of 300 in six weeks. Sperrle refused to believe this estimate, asserting that Dowding still had 1,000 fighters, but Kesselring, whose planes had done most of the fighting, was ready to believe that Fighter Command was on its last legs. The Reichsmarschall [Göring] agreed with him. The question of how to induce the RAF to commit its remaining fighters to a decisive final battle remained. The answer seemed to lie in a mass assault on London, which the British must defend if they were to avoid the crushing bombardment which had broken Warsaw and Rotterdam.[5]

By forcing Dowding to commit all his strength to the defence of the capital, both Göring and Kesselring believed this would enable the Bf 109s to engage and destroy the British fighters, thereby finishing off Fighter Command once and for all.

As such an assault could only have been launched with the permission of the Führer, Göring promptly sought his consent. As Denis Richards explains:

It would, of course, be too much to see in these [RAF] raids on Berlin the whole cause of Hitler's next move; but they unquestionably added to his anger at the activities of Bomber Command. What better policy, then, for this final phase, than to enjoy a swift and sweet revenge by hurling the Luftwaffe in force against London? For if the British capital could be reduced to chaos, the task of the invading [German] armies would be enormously simplified; indeed, if Göring's pilots did their work well enough, the need for a military expedition might entirely disappear. And nothing could be more agreeable than to be freed from the necessity of crossing the Channel while the Royal Navy and the Royal Air Force were still in being.

Hitler accordingly informed the world that his patience was once more exhausted. 'The British', he declared, 'drop their bombs indiscriminately and without plan on civilian residential quarters and farms and villages. For three months I did not reply because I believed that they would stop, but in this Mr. Churchill saw a sign

3. See Martin Middlebrook and Chris Everitt, *The Bomber Command War Diaries; An Operational Reference Book 1939-1945* (Pen & Sword, Barnsley, 2014).
4. Denis Richards, *Royal Air Force 1939-1945*, Vol.1 (HMSO, London, 1953), pp.182–4.
5. Michael Glover, *Invasion Scare 1940* (Leo Cooper, London, 1990), pp.159–60.

Above: A balloon barrage flies over factories and industrial buildings in Liverpool before or during the Blitz. (National Museum of Denmark)

Right: Located on Fore Street, within the modern Barbican complex, St Giles-without-Cripplegate Church was one of the first buildings within the City of London to be badly damaged during the war – in this case during a raid on the evening of 24 August 1940, before the official start of the Blitz. Here, ARP personnel are pictured at work in the aftermath of the attack. (Historic Military Press)

of our weakness. The British will know that we are now giving our answer night after night. We shall stop the handiwork of these night pilots.'

Hitler's permission for the Luftwaffe to strike at the very heart of London was duly given on 5 September. 'Three days later…', concluded Richards, 'the Luftwaffe abandoned its offensive against the sector stations and began the assault on London. From the point of view of winning the battle [of Britain], Dowding himself could not have made a more satisfactory decision.'

That same day, the 5th, the Luftwaffe high command, Oberkommando der Luftwaffe (OKL), issued the orders for a force of over 300 bombers, with massive fighter cover, to attack the docks in London's East End on the afternoon of 7 September. However, the signal relaying these instructions was intercepted by the 'Y' Service, a chain of wireless intercept stations across Britain and in a number of countries overseas. Decoded by personnel working on the *Ultra* programme at the Government Code and Cypher School at Bletchley Park, details regarding Göring's signal were soon in the hands of the Prime Minister and Dowding.[6]

Göring, though, could not have been more wrong. Fighter Command and all its support services had battled through the weeks of adversity and, relatively speaking, stood as strong as ever. It had indeed proven to be, as Churchill had predicted, the nation's finest hour. But, as Britain's leaders now knew, if not the people themselves, an even greater test of the nation's character lay ahead.

A Historic Moment

Dawn on 7 September, the day that the Luftwaffe was to execute Göring's master plan, brought another bright, clear, late summer's day – ideal flying conditions.

Having decided to witness the day's events first-hand, the Reichsmarschall had travelled in his own personal train, named *Robinson*, to northern France. Accompanied by Generalfeldmarschall Kesselring, General der Flieger Bruno Lörzer, commander of II Fliegerkorps, and other senior officers, he made his way to the clifftop at Cap Gris-Nez to watch the German aircraft form up and pass overhead en route for London.

With the Luftwaffe bombers on their way, Göring returned to his train to finalise a speech for the German people that he intended to be broadcast later that day. When aired, it included the following introduction by an announcer:

The moment facing each of us here in this place again is one which we shall never forget. This hour has seen our own plane crews assembled within a few kilometres of the English capital, and striking for the first time at the enemy's heart… The Reichsmarschall is leaving his train and coming past us. He sees us. Is this what he was intending? Is he really coming? Yes. He is coming! The Reichsmarschall is coming from his train and is coming to the microphone.

Göring himself then spoke:

I now want to take this opportunity of speaking to you, to say this moment is a historic one. As a result of the provocative British attacks on Berlin on recent nights, the Führer has decided to order a mighty blow to be struck

in revenge against the capital of the British Empire. I personally have assumed the leadership of this attack, and today I have heard above me the roaring of the victorious German squadrons which now, for the first time, are driving towards the heart of the

A black 'S' air raid shelter sign that, painted on a white background, can still be seen on a wall in Frankham Street, Deptford, London. As indicated, the shelter entrance was 50 yards away. (Courtesy of Robert Mitchell)

6. John Terraine, *Right of the Line* (Hodder & Stoughton, London, 1985), p.207.

Above left: A Luftwaffe photograph taken during an attack on Tilbury Docks, on the Thames Estuary, with clouds of dust and debris rising from the explosions. (National Museum of Denmark)

Above right: A second photograph taken from a Luftwaffe bombing during an attack on Tilbury Docks on the Thames Estuary. (National Museum of Denmark)

Below: A fire lights up the night sky over London after a lone German bomber had dropped incendiary bombs close to the heart of the city on 1 September 1940. (Historic Military Press)

enemy in full daylight, accompanied by countless fighter squadrons. Enemy defences were, as we expected, beaten down and the target reached, and I am certain that our successes have been as massive as the boldness of our plan of attack and the fighting spirit of our crews deserve. In any event this is an historic hour, in which for the first time the German Luftwaffe has struck at the heart of the enemy.[7]

The Bombers Approach

With the Luftwaffe preparing for the change in its tactics, the aerial activity so far on the 7th had been subdued, to say the least. As Ian Jones MBE explains:

For the weary Battle of Britain pilots waiting anxiously by their aircraft, there was immense relief that most of the telephones which would dispatch them into the air remained silent. The staff in the 11 Group Control Room and the Sector Headquarters were also puzzled by the lack of activity; clearly something was brewing, but what? With the constant attacks on the RAF's airfields, there was concern that the Germans were beginning to get the upper hand in the struggle for air superiority in the southeast of the country. It was not until late afternoon that the first ominous blips on the radar screens gave an indication that a concentrated force of aircraft was being assembled for a raid. It must have been just before 17.00 hours that it became clear that this was no ordinary raid. Such a concentrated and mighty force could only have one target and that was London. The head of Fighter Command, Dowding, and his Group Commander, Keith Park, quickly realized this. But for the population of London, despite the air raid

Heinkel He 111s are pictured landing back at their base in France having attacked targets in Britain in the summer of 1940. (National Museum of Denmark)

7. Winston G. Ramsey (Ed.), *The Blitz Then and Now: Volume 2* (Battle of Britain Prints International, London, 1988), p.45.

Right: A Dornier Do 17 drops its deadly cargo on a British target. According to the original caption, this image was taken over the Thames Estuary, possibly during the attack on Thameshaven. (National Museum of Denmark)

Below: Perhaps contemplating their forthcoming missions to London, a pair of German aircrew are pictured 'looking towards the English Channel coast' from northern France during the summer of 1940. (National Museum of Denmark)

sirens, which some people now ignored, there was no such appreciation. Away to the east, the Luftwaffe aircraft massed in a huge, phalanx-shaped formation, which was stepped from 14,000 to 23,000 feet. It advanced on a twenty-mile front towards the Thames Estuary. Like a relentless juggernaut the bombers bore down on the capital. Though harried by more and more Spitfires and Hurricanes, the protective screen of Messerschmitts mostly held them at bay and the British fighters were unable to seriously blunt or deflect the bomber force. Below and ahead of them the people of London, and those in the East End in particular, had no idea of what was about to befall them.[8]

William Thompson was part of the Air Raid Precautions (ARP) services in Woolwich:

We got the red alert as was often the case when an impending raid was approaching from the Thames Estuary. But the usual practice was for the bomber formations to split up near the Isle of Sheppy and they then set course for the RAF aerodromes north and south of the Thames; then we would revert back to a yellow [alert]. But in this case, we were under a 'red' for longer than usual and messages started to come in that the bombers were seen coming up the Thames.

Well, I went up and I have never seen anything like it. A thick blanket of black bombers which must have been two miles wide following the Thames. Our station was almost at the road junction that now goes down to the Woolwich ferry, and we had an excellent view of what was going to happen. I think the first bombs were dropped just before the dock areas and the right side of the formation would pass right over us. We could do nothing but get back to our posts and pray like mad. The sound was deafening, the building shook and dust from walls and ceilings started to envelope our desks, we could do nothing while the raid was on, although a few phone calls came through, 'this street got it' and 'so and so building has got a direct hit'. Then silence, slowly the phones died, lines had been cut.

The Luftwaffe's attack on London was scheduled to begin at 17.00 hours, and the 348 bombers and 617 fighters bore down on the British capital right on time. 'I'd never seen so many aircraft in the air all at the same time', remembered Squadron Leader Sandy Johnstone of the Spitfire-equipped 602 (City of Glasgow) Squadron. 'It was a hazy sort of day to about 16,000 feet. As we broke through the haze, you could hardly believe it. As far as you could see, there was nothing but German aircraft coming in, wave after wave.'

As the enemy had steadily converged in one direction for an hour and a half, no less than 21 of the 23 squadrons that had been scrambled and sent up succeeded in engaging. The German losses were therefore heavy – 40 aircraft against 28 of the defending fighters. The powerful escorts, however, had safeguarded the German bombers, and nearly all the machines shot down by the RAF pilots were fighters. The bombers, on the whole, continued to push on towards the Thames. The most concentrated enemy force arrayed against the United Kingdom since the Spanish Armada was about to unleash a deadly attack, the likes of which had never been seen before on British soil.

---

8. Ian Jones MBE, *London - Bombed, Blitzed and Blown Up: The British Capital Under Attack Since 1867* (Frontline, Barnsley, 2016), p.175.

Chapter 3

Black Saturday

Lieutenant Alan Rook was serving on a searchlight post just to the east of London when he heard the unmistakable sound of anti-aircraft fire. Suddenly, his commanding officer burst into his office shouting, 'My God, they've started'. Both men ran outside to obverse the events unfolding around them. 'Coming up the river in close order', Rook recalled, 'was the biggest fleet of aeroplanes I had ever seen. White against the blue sky, like cherry blossoms seen from below, in level rows of squadrons, hundreds strong, filling the air with a throbbing roar, they came very slowly, following the river towards London.'[1]

The writer Virginia Cowles was staying at the home of a British press magnate, Esmond Harmsworth, in the Kent village of Mereworth, about 30 miles southeast of central London. Along with a friend, she was having tea on the lawn, enjoying the late

Luftwaffe groundcrew and armourers bombing up a Heinkel He 111 in preparation for a sortie over Britain. (National Museum of Denmark)

afternoon warmth and sun, when a low rumble gradually rose from the southeast. 'At first we couldn't see anything', Cowles later wrote, 'but soon the noise had grown into a deep, full roar, like the faraway thunder of a giant waterfall'. She and her friend counted more than 150 aircraft, the bombers flying in formation, with fighters surrounding them in a protective shield. 'We lay in the grass, our eyes strained towards the sky; we made out a batch of tiny white specks, like clouds of insects moving northwest in the direction of the capital.'[2]

A young Colin Perry was bicycling over Chipstead Hill. On hearing the increasingly loud sound of aircraft overhead he glanced up to see whether they were fighters or bombers. 'It was the most amazing, impressive, riveting sight. Directly above me were literally hundreds of planes, Germans! The sky was full of them. Bombers hemmed in with fighters, like bees around their queen, like destroyers round the battleship, so came Jerry.'[3]

Forming a block described as being '20 miles wide', the German bombers were also observed by Harold Nicolson and Vita Sackville-West, who were, like Cowles, taking tea in the garden of their country house in Kent. The attackers were, Nicolson confirmed, 'coming over in wave after wave'. Farther west, in the countryside just outside London, the American newspaperman Ben Robertson watched the bombers as they 'flew at a very great height, glistening like beautiful steel birds in the afternoon sunshine'.[4]

---

1. Norman Moss, *Nineteen Weeks: America, Britain, and the Fateful Summer of 1940* (Houghton Mifflin, New York, 2003), p.305.
2. Quoted on www.medium.com/@dennisbranson.mentor2016.
3. Quoted in Philip Ziegler, *London at War* (Knopf, New York, 1995), p.113.
4. Benjamin Schwarz, 'Black Saturday', in *The Atlantic*, April 2008 issue.

Above left: **Oberleutnant Erwin Daig, on the right, and a colleague pose for a photograph on their airfield in Northern France earlier in the Battle of Britain. (Historic Military Press)**

Above right: **Daig's Messerschmitt Bf 109 is seen here on display during the War Weapons Week in Nuneaton, Warwickshire. (Historic Military Press)**

'The Chase Was Finally Over'

One of the many pilots heading towards London that afternoon was Oberleutnant Erwin Daig of 5/JG 27. At the controls of his Messerschmitt Bf 109E-1, Daig, along with the rest of his Staffel, was to provide part of the bombers' escorts for the opening wave of the Blitz. He takes up the story himself, providing an insight into the aerial combats that raged over southern England on 7 September:

Having taken off, we quickly took up our assembly positions with the bombers in the skies over St. Omer. A direct course was then set for London. I was one of about 40 Bf-109s, though not all of the fighters were from JG 27. On the approach flight we first made contact with the enemy to the south of the city [London]. Here we mixed with English fighters, there being a fair amount of activity and many short aerial combats. Having dropped our bombs, the formation set course for the French Channel coast. However, somewhere in

An artist's impression of the last minutes of Oberleutnant Erwin Daig's Messerschmitt Bf 109 E-1. Daig made an emergency landing on a private pre-war airstrip at Charity Farm in the small West Sussex village of Cootham. (Historic Military Press)

the earlier attacks I must have been hit for I could not maintain the prescribed speed. As a result of this, and the fact that I had been the last outer right plane, I had begun to trail well behind the rest of the formation. My radio transmitter had also packed up, as I could get no answer from the formation to my calls. I then made a mistake that was going to cost me my freedom. Instead of going into a glide, assisted by the engine, and trying to reach the French coast, I maintained my height. At this point, two British fighters who had dived down at me from behind on my left-hand side, and from a higher altitude, attacked me. They opened fire, and my plane received more hits. As they did this one of the attackers, possibly a Spitfire, flew past me on my left side. I tried to fire at it and then turned into a steep dive. During this dive I lost contact with my attackers. As I headed over Southern England towards France I tried to reach some broken cloud that I could see at about 3,000 metres. This was another tactical mistake, as before I reached the safety of this cloud. One of my attackers caught up with me and again opened fire. Once again I felt the shock of more hits, at which point I put my plane into yet another dive. This time I kept going until I was almost at ground level, when I headed straight for France, trying to escape by flying at low level. This went on for a short time. With occasional hits on me by the pursuer. By now my plane had started to smoke, and I was having trouble seeing. I threw back my cockpit hood to see if this would help, but all that happened was that the engine just died! I then saw a gently rising slope, similar to a meadow, that was profusely covered with old lorries. I quickly lost speed and then the plane hit the ground. The chase was finally over.[5]

Hit in the cooling system, Daig's was one the 24 German aircraft brought down over the United Kingdom on 7 September; at the time the Ministry of Home Security claimed 88 aircraft destroyed. Of this number, only four were bombers. This suggests that Fighter Command's pilots were drawn away from the bombers by their escorts. The majority of the former, therefore, battled their way through to the target.

Over the East End

It was at 16.43 hours, on 7 September, that the sirens in London sounded on that fateful Saturday afternoon. Following the undulating wail of the sirens, often referred to unflatteringly as 'Wailing Winnie', 'Moaning Minnie' or the 'Sighreen', came the chilling throb of aero engines as the sky filled with ominous black shapes.

Alan Fry was an ambulance man stationed at the ARP depot and ambulance station in Abbey Road in Newham. He was part way through a 24-hour shift when the sirens went off:

The air-raid warning went, and we were all looking up in the sky and we saw a black mass of planes coming over. Everybody was shouting out, 'That's alright, they're our planes' and before we could say any more they started bombing us. I made a dive under my ambulance. The next thing I know, the whole place came down on top of us. We were completely buried. One bomb had penetrated the back of the building. I could just see the daylight through the dust. I realised that I couldn't walk properly – something had happened to my leg. My helmet had been blown off. I managed to crawl over to this hole. When I got out, it was chaos. Everything was alight and there were craters everywhere. There were tons of sulphur alight at Berk's [Chemical Works], which was next door. I seemed to be the only one to get out.[6]

Above left: Palls of smoke rise over the docks and East End on 7 September 1940. The original caption, dated 23 September, states: 'German bombs fire the London dock area. German sources say that this aerial picture shows the effects "of the first big concerted attack of the German air force on London Dock and industry districts".' (National Museum of Denmark)

Above right: A view of the British countryside as seen from the cockpit of a Heinkel He 111 during the summer of 1940. (Historic Military Press)

5. Quoted in Martin Mace, *The Chanctonbury Crashes* (Historic Military Press, Storrington, 1998), pp.16–7.
6. 'Black Saturday: Stories From The First Day of the Blitz', a leaflet produced by London Borough of Newham Heritage & Archives.

Thirteen men were killed at the Abbey Road depot in this incident.

A young Donald Wharf had been playing in the garden of his family home, 'digging away at the sunbaked soil, making a trench for my soldiers', when the raiders appeared in the sky over Newham:

I sat there transfixed by the grey puffs of smoke that were gathering high in the sky; then they began to move closer. Somebody yelled, 'Look, anti-aircraft fire' – that was when dad, and then my mother, appeared and whisked me away to the shelter. The noise from outside was getting steadily louder and louder. Then they were right overhead – our ears were bombarded with sounds: gunfire, the throbbing of enemy aircraft, but worse, the 'crunch' of their bombs. Slowly though, after a massive explosion, it all simply faded away. What was no more than a lull in the storm, soon ended and more Dorniers came in another great wave – their bombs crashing all round us. I wished it would end but the bombers kept coming – dozens and dozens it seemed, dropping their bombs more or less as they pleased.[7]

First Trip to the Cinema

For a young John Matthews, the afternoon of 7 September was meant to be a special one – it was to be his first ever visit to the cinema. Accompanied by his parents, he made his way to the Odeon in Woolwich in see *The Bluebird*, starring Shirley Temple. Unfortunately, the cinema was a short distance up the road from Woolwich Ferry, opposite the Royal Docks, and close to the main gate of Woolwich Arsenal – right in the crosshairs of the German bombsights.

It was the early evening performance so we must have got to the cinema at about four o'clock… The film had just started when a caption appeared on the screen to warn the audience that the sirens had sounded. A few people got up and walked out, but most stayed put. We had paid some 9d (3p) for our seats and did not want to throw good money away. The noise of the air-raid soon drowned out the film. We could hear bombers overhead and bombs exploding nearby, the rattle of anti-aircraft fire, but most worrying were the bells and sirens on the fire-engines and ambulances that roared past on the main road outside… Then a stick of incendiary bombs came through the roof… I can remember a lot of vivid white smoke and there was a peculiar smell, which was probably the burning magnesium in the bombs. Then there was total pandemonium. People were screaming and rushing for the doors. I saw people on fire.

After sheltering in the cinema for a while, Jack and his parents made their way out into the street, at which point they were greeted by an unforgettable sight:

There were wrecked and burning buildings all around, and an orange glow in the sky almost turned night into day. From St. Paul's for a distance of about nine miles down the river virtually every building was ablaze. On the other side of the river, a little higher up the Thames, a warehouse was burning. As we watched its wall slumped down into the water. There were barges drifting down the Thames on fire. There was also a sickly, sweet smell, which, I have since learnt, was probably burning sugar in the warehouses. Then we walked up toward the main crossroads. I saw a boot in the road with something sticking out of it and paused to look. My mother dragged me away saying, 'It's only an old shoe.' But it wasn't: it was a shiny-new boot with part of someone's leg in it. At Beresford Square a tram appeared miraculously. We jumped aboard. I can remember the sound of the metal wheels grinding the broken glass in the street as we went along.

It turned out that the tram only covered some 200 yards before being brought to halt by the many firemen's hoses laid out in the road. 'We had to walk some five miles home', concluded John, 'and didn't arrive till just before dawn'.[8]

---

7. ibid.
8. BBC People's War website, Article ID: A3559656.

Above left: The attacks at the beginning of September introduced a new experience to many Londoners – that of spending their nights in the capital's underground stations. (Library of Congress)

Above right: Buckingham Palace was first hit on 8 September 1940, when a 50kg delayed-action high explosive bomb landed harmlessly in the grounds. Damage was caused the following day, when a swimming pool was all but destroyed, and then on the 13th, when this image was taken. During the second of three daylight attacks that day, a raider dropped a stick of five bombs on the Palace, one of which struck and damaged the Royal Chapel – seen here. (Historic Military Press)

Right: The source of so much destruction was the Luftwaffe's 1kg incendiary. (Historic Military Press)

GERMAN BOMB B 2·2 EI-Z
(ANTI PERSONNEL INCENDIARY BOMB)

Doris Lilian Bennett also remembered that weekend only too well:

That Saturday was a warm, sunny Autumn day. In the late afternoon, we of the Auxiliary Fire Service, stationed at the London Fire Brigade Station at the bottom end of the Isle of Dogs, were standing in the Station yard watching the vapour trails of aircraft high in the sky when it was suggested we might get a better view from an upstairs window. Watching from the window towards Greenwich, across the Thames, we suddenly saw aircraft approaching, quite low, their shapes black against the bright sky. We watched, mesmerised, until someone said, uneasily, 'I think we'd better go downstairs, these blokes look like they mean business'. They did. We closed the window and were walking, unhurriedly, down the stairs when suddenly came loud rushing noises and huge explosions. Bombs! We were being bombed![9]

9. BBC People's War website, Article ID: A2613241.

Workmen repair a crater that was made in a road at Elephant and Castle during the bombing on 7/8 September 1940. (NARA)

Nearby, in Poplar, 18-year-old Len Jones stared up at the mass of aircraft. 'The first formations were coming over without any bombs dropping', he remembered, 'but very, very majestic; terrific. And I had no thought that they were actually bombers.'

Poplar had been selected by the Luftwaffe as one of the targets because of its warehouses and gas works, and visibility was good in the late afternoon sunshine. Len Jones was very soon only too aware that they were indeed bombers:

> Bombs began to fall, and shrapnel was going along King Street, dancing off the cobbles. Then the real impetus came, in so far as the suction and the compression from the high explosive blasts just pulled you and pushed you, and the whole of this atmosphere was turbulating [*sic*] so hard that, after an explosion of a nearby bomb, you could actually feel your eyeballs being sucked out. I was holding my eyes to try and stop them going. And the suction was so vast, it ripped my shirt away, and ripped my trousers. Then I couldn't get my breath, the smoke was like acid and everything round me was black and yellow. And these bombers just kept on and on, the whole road was moving, rising and falling.[10]

One of those who witnessed the opening attack of the Blitz, in his case from the relative (at that stage) safety of central London, was the American military attaché, General Raymond E Lee. He recorded his observations of wartime London in a journal, and this included his description of the attack on 7 September:

> About five o'clock, an air raid warning went but those of us who had stayed behind on a hot Saturday afternoon to try and catch up with our correspondence paid no attention. However, at a quarter to six I heard some antiaircraft guns cracking away in the distance and then a series of heavy explosions to the northeast and not as far away. They kept on, and at the same time the droning of planes overhead increased, and I

---

10. Joanna Mack and Steve Humphries, *London at War: The Making of Modern London, 1939-1945* (Sidgwick & Jackson, London, 1985), p.40.

went out on the square where I could see little flecks like bits of tinfoil darting about overhead, so high that they were almost out of sight. Only an occasional burst of machine-gun fire showed that fierce combat was going on in the heavens. Then McDonald, who had been on the roof, came down and reported that great fires were raging as a result of the bombardment. We went up. Over beyond the Houses of Parliament, a huge mushroom of billowing smoke had risen so high as to blot out the sky and the barrage balloons, which float at about five thousand feet. In the heart of it, fierce red glows showed that immense fires were raging. McDonald had counted about two hundred planes in the attack, which was made with a vigor and a force hitherto unused by the Germans against London.

Lee was determined to inspect the aftermath of the German attack close-up:

As it looked as though the actual bombing was over, although the guns in Hyde Park were cracking away at a few stragglers, I got a taxi and drove towards the fire… People outside were resuming their ordinary activities… People were reading papers and flirting in St. James's Park. Commuters were running for their trains at Waterloo. The fires seemed to be further and further away but a torrent of fire apparatus, raging past, showed us the way. Finally, we arrived at the Tower and from Tower Bridge one could look down the Thames and see immense fires raging on both sides of the river. I had to park the taxi here and walk down through the streets of Wapping, crowded with fire apparatus, police and soldiers establishing picket lines, not to mention all the riverside and slum population of the neighborhood. Tremendous fires were raging within a block of where these crowds were, but they displayed little excitement and no signs of panic.[11]

'An Ominous Brightness'

From the roof of the Home Office building in Whitehall, Wing Commander John Hodsoll, the Inspector General of Air Raid Precautions, watched the unfolding drama: 'Huge clouds of black smoke were billowing and spiralling up into the clear blue sky; great spurts of flame were shooting up; there was a dull thud of bombs as they exploded and reverberated in the distance, and an acrid smell of burning was borne in on the wind. The docks looked as if they had been reduced to one great inferno.'

The raid lasted for approximately an hour, the 'All Clear' being sounded at 18.10 hours. During those frantic 60-or-so minutes, the devastation wrought of parts of London had been enormous. Factory buildings had been demolished, hundreds of tons of timber had been left in charred ruin, warehouses filled with foodstuffs and other supplies vital to the war effort had gone up in smoke and the houses of the dockers and the little corner shops that fed them had collapsed into rubble.

The famous Welsh poet and writer Dylan Thomas was in London that day along with the cookery writer, model, and actress Theodora FitzGibbon. During the late afternoon raid, the pair drank their way through the bombing, firstly with wine at the home of Theodora's friend and artist Peter Pulham, and then they finished off at The King's Head & Eight Bells public house in Cheyne Walk, Chelsea:

At about six-thirty the 'all clear' sounded and by then the sky was the colour of a blood orange, a seething flaming mass… After a year of blackout it was weird to have light again, but it was an ominous brightness… Inside the pub, everybody was speculating as to what had happened on this sunny, Saturday, September afternoon. Jokes were made to relieve the tension; beer mugs were put down more noisily to shut down other sounds. We were glued together by dread. All our eyes were rounder, the pupils enlarged, and although we laughed, our lips twitched with alarm… We did not know it then, but the winter of bombs, or the Blitz as it was called, had begun.[12]

11. James Leutze (Ed.), *The London Observer: The Journal of General Raymond E. Lee 1940-1941* (Hutchinson, London, 1972), p.47.
12. Peter Stansky, *The First Day of the Blitz* (Yale University Press, London, 2007), pp.168–9.

Chapter 4

The Bombers Return

L ike so many others, when the 'All Clear' sounded at about 18.10 hours on September 7, Barbara Nixon believed that the terrors of the day were over, and she went off to dinner. But, barely a couple of hours later, the bombers were back. 'When we came out of the restaurant [in Soho] we stopped aghast', Nixon recalled. 'The whole of the sky to the east was blazing red. The afternoon spectacle was completely dwarfed; it seemed as though half of London must be burning… I realized that the whole of London was a target area, and that Piccadilly and King's Cross were as important as the Albert Dock, and any street might get its share.'

Some 250 Heinkels and Dorniers found easy targets, with the fires from the earlier raids illuminating the ground through the heavy smoke that still chocked the air. It was until 04.30 hours the following morning that the droning procession went on. It was as Göring's second wave was being unleashed on London that Ida Nash disembarked from a train at Willesden. A worker with the Post Office, her department had been moved out of London to Morecambe. She had been granted a period of leave and was intent on going home to be with her parents at 48 Sandford Road, East Ham, in the heart of the East End.

The train from Blackpool was already two hours late when it arrived at Willesden at about 20.10 hours. As it could get no further because of the earlier attack, the train was emptied there. 'It was here', wrote Ida to a friend the following day, 'that we got our first taste of Jerry. Over to the south-east there was a horrible red glow in the sky, and I might as well admit that my knees started feeling appallingly weak especially as at that precise moment the sirens started wailing.'[1]

Londoners awake the morning after the night raid to find their streets strewn with fire hoses abandoned by the exhausted fire and ARP personnel. (Historic Military Press)

---

1. Department of Documents, Imperial War Museum, Reference 99/66/1.

Above left: German bombers cross the French coast bound for Britain. The image was taken by an officer who served in the 3rd Battery, Reserve Flak Regiment 405. From 7 July 1940, the unit's guns were emplaced in positions in the Creil, Quiberville and Boulogne areas. (Historic Military Press)

Above right: As the fires rage, a fireman on an extendable ladder works to put out the flames engulfing one building. (Historic Military Press)

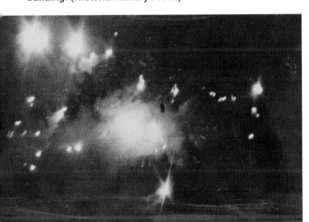

Above left: A view of London under attack during a night raid in the Blitz. (National Museum of Denmark)

Above right: A view of bomb damage in Threadneedle Street, in the City, taken on the morning of 8 September 1940. The damage was the result of the bombing the previous day and night. (Historic Military Press)

In what she described as 'literally inky blackness', Ida managed to catch the Tube to Euston Station, where she had arranged to meet her mother, but the place was virtually deserted. She went out to the road, hoping to catch a bus: 'The fire was getting steadily brighter, and overhead there were sounds of gunfire and the occasional dull thud in the distance as the bombs dropped. I've never felt so desperately alone in all my life.'

Ida walked on. She managed to get as far as Euston Square Station, but when she tried to buy a ticket for East Ham, she was told that there were no trains beyond Bow Street – that station had been hit and Stepney Green station had also been severely damaged. There was nothing for it but try and catch a bus. So, along with some 20 others, Ida waited at the bus stop.

A few taxis came by, but no bus. Then, remarkably, her mother walked past right in front of Ida! She had been turned away from Euston at 20.30 hours and, as the raid was still in progress, she had started to walk home. Even though she had already walked from Euston Station, Ida's mother immediately suggested that they should walk home – through the streets in the height of the second wave of German bombers.

I was already swaying on my feet from tiredness and I was famished into the bargain, not having had a solid meal since breakfast, yet I said 'OK' and off we went. I think that if we'd both been feeling hale and hearty, we wouldn't have gone but we seemed so numbed that nothing much mattered. Before we'd gone far, things began to happen. The whole of Thames-side from London Bridge to Woolwich was a raging inferno. You could have seen to read by the light and unfortunately for us we had to go by the East India Docks. Commercial Road was the only route open to the East because, owing to the damage done by Bow Road, traffic was being diverted from there. And just before we got to Burdett Road the bombs started falling. The shelters seemed to be absolutely non-existent, so we just went on. One plane in particular was determined to get a big chimney-stack near where we were walking, and bombs just fell in rapid succession… What was so maddening was the persistent drone of enemy planes which are easily distinguishable from our own. We couldn't get away from it, and felt so completely helpless. Fires were breaking out everywhere, and once a chapel that lay back about thirty yards from us on the other side of the road suddenly burst into flames before our eyes. It was dreadful.

'Fear was the Predominant Emotion'

The fire brigades across London had trained for just such an attack, but putting that into action was a different matter altogether, as Auxiliary Fireman Stephen Spender found out: 'The street water mains, totally inadequate to carry the vast quantities of water needed to control fires of such magnitude, were further depleted when sections fractured under the pounding of exploding bombs. Those firemen working on dockyard fires were fortunate in having an almost unlimited supply of water to draw on but watched their powerful jets bore into the mass of flames without visible effect.'[2]

Some of the experienced regular firemen had witnessed fires of similar intensity, but never on such an overwhelming scale. 'The choking fumes from burning rubber and tar; the blistering heat and blinding sparks were merely unpleasant incidentals; fear was the predominant emotion that drew branchmen together in small groups, each gaining comfort from the presence of the other. Many feared their last hour had come.'

Civil Defence teams moved into action as well, many for the first time, also witnessing scenes they could scarcely come to terms with. Though reeling with shock and horror, they were swiftly scouring damaged buildings for survivors, as a young Arsenal supporter recalled, having returned from a match against their fierce rivals Spurs. The sirens announcing the first raid had been ignored by the players and spectators alike, and the game continued for its full 90 minutes. Young Jack and his dad returned home safely:

[But] after a short time towards evening the sirens went off again and we all went downstairs to the ground floor I then heard a bomb whistling down and the house collapsed on top of us. I laid conscious for several hours with the lady from downstairs screaming with pain and trying to move which gave me considerable pain. I then heard digging and then felt some air and a hand touched me and was then subsequently dug out and taken to Mile End Hospital.

Jack and his father survived but not his mother. The men who dug him out of the ruins of his house told him that one day he would get his revenge; and he did – he joined the RAF.[3]

Jack's mother was one of the many who could not be saved that night. All too often, a collapsed building formed the poignant backdrop to heart-rending scenes as survivors uncovered the mutilated remains of loved ones. First aid teams tended the living, but for the dead there was nothing they could do other than cover the bodies with blankets, leaving them in the streets to await collection by a mortuary van.

It had been drummed into those first aiders that above all they had to be aseptic and how important it was for them to scrub their hands before treating anyone. But all such precautions went to the wind as tremendous amounts of dust and dirt was blown into the sky from the detonations of the bombs and the crumbling masonry only to land back on the streets and on the first aiders and the people they were treating.

Amid that dust-filled air, fire belched skywards from gas mains in the streets, fire hoses were stretched across pavements and over rubble, and the sirens of ambulances echoed unremittingly around the demolished buildings as the raid continued throughout the night. From 20.00 hours on the 7th through to

---

2. Cyril Demarne, *The London Blitz, A Fireman's Tale* (After the Battle, London, 1991), p.19.
3. BBC People's War website, Article ID: A4378610.

Firemen spray water on damaged and still smouldering buildings near London Bridge, in the City of London, on the morning of 9 September 1940. (Historic Military Press)

04.00 hours the following morning, some 250 bombers kept up a slow, agonizing procession over the British capital. Between them, they dropped some 300 tons of high explosive and 13,000 incendiaries, rather more than their comrades had dropped during the first wave.

Police and air raid wardens were busy all night and into the following morning trying to keep people away from buildings that were liable to collapse or had an unexploded bomb buried in their ruins; and ruins were everywhere across the East End. Clustered round the docks were the badly built houses of the poor, and thousands of residences were destroyed. Many East Enders, already on the lower strata of society, lost everything they possessed.

Death in the Shelters

Even those who had sought refuge in the many air raid shelters around London suffered at the hand of the bombers that night. Emma Williams was a civil defence worker in Stepney during the night of 7/8 September:

> We were directed to go to a shelter that had been engulfed in fire during the evening raid, but we had to cease operations when the night raids got too heavy. We returned at about four o'clock the following morning to see what we could do. A number of people had managed to get out of the shelter, but they reported to us that there were people still inside and that some of them were dead. As we pulled heavy beams out of the way and carefully removed large pieces of timber we were stopped once again when it was reported that someone had found an unexploded bomb. The Royal Engineers were called in, and we were told that these UXBs (unexploded bombs) were actually delayed action bombs that were due to explode about ten hours after they had been dropped. It was about midday before we again went in and tried to excavate the area around the shelter. We knew that there was now no hope of finding anybody alive, but one never knows. Stranger things have happened. When we finally got down to the shelter, we found body over body, people almost burnt to a cinder: the air smelt of burning flesh that had gone rotten. I could take no more and had to get out, I was proud of the job I was doing, but on this occasion I was not afraid to call myself a coward, I just could not do it, but like so many others I plucked up courage to go back later. But the situation was absolutely shocking.[4]

Scenes such as those witnessed by Emma Williams were experienced first-hand by 12-year-old Tom Betts. In the aftermath of the first wave of raiders, he had persuaded his mother that they were safer in an official shelter nearby – the Columbia Market Shelter, a large site that had previously been used as storage under the market in Bethnal Green:

> We were not too familiar with the shelter and had only used it once before, when there was light bombing. It was large – about one and a half football pitches in size, divided it into two equal parts by a wall. We had

---

4. Quoted on www.battleofbritain1940.net/0037.html

Accompanied by Winston Churchill, King George VI and Queen Elizabeth inspect bomb damage at Buckingham Palace on 10 September 1940. (Historic Military Press)

Above left: Damage caused to the Inner Temple Library during a night attack in the first few days of the Blitz in September 1940. The Inner Temple Library, a legal reference library that dated back to 1506, would suffer further damage. One source states that, 'The building was destroyed during the Second World War: several thousand volumes of printed books (but none of the manuscripts) were lost. The destroyed books were mostly replaced, either by gift or purchase, over the next 30 years or so.' (Historic Military Press)

Above right: The aftermath of a bomb falling through all the floors of one London apartment block in the first few days of the Blitz in September 1940. (Historic Military Press)

all been given the luxury of a sheet of corrugated metal to sleep on. The shelter began to get warmer and, with over a hundred people down there, it became very hot. Everyone was calm and in one spot there was a wedding party going on they were laughing and singing. The noise outside told us all that bombs were falling and the occasional rumble indicated they were getting closer. As the night went on, I must have fallen asleep, but I remember feeling very uncomfortable and hearing my mother next to me, chatting to my aunt. All that I can recollect after that was feeling giddy and sick. Still feeling very giddy, I opened my eyes. It was dark. I could hear screams and whistles. Startled, I remembered where I was and began to feel around for my mother and brother, as it was impossible to see. The air was full of dust and it was pitch black. In the far distance I could see a tiny light from a small bulb. I could not get my bearings. Still lying on the ground, I focused on the dim glow coming from that bulb in the distance. It was hanging above the exit doors. As I neared the light, I realised fully what had happened and remembered that within the shelter was a First Aid room, as I had been to it as a volunteer to be bandaged up weeks earlier. So, instead of going into the street, I pushed my way towards the First Aid room and, after I nearly forced the door, they let me in. Inside, there were about twenty people including one of my friends. A nurse bandaged my head and we sat in there for what seemed like hours.[5]

Tom, still without his mother and brother, was eventually transported to hospital to have his wounds checked. It transpired that a single German bomb had fallen down the ventilation shaft and exploded inside the shelter. A total of 45 people were killed outright, or subsequently died of their wounds. Whilst Tom was eventually reunited with his brother, it was discovered that his mother was one of those who had been fatally injured: 39-year-old Dorothy May Betts died of her wounds on 17 September.

Moved into Danger

When the summer holidays began in the summer of 1940, a young Bill Morris, who had previously been evacuated to Worthing on the South Coast in September 1939, returned home to his parent's flat in Rotherhithe New Road. The road, unfortunately for Bill and his family, connected Surrey Commercial Docks to the Old Kent Road.

The first inkling of the trouble to come on 7 September was when the anti-aircraft guns in the nearby Southwark Park opened up, followed soon after by the growl of the approaching German bombers. 'Shortly after this', remembers Bill, 'the sunny afternoon was shattered by the crunch of exploding bombs nearby as the strong smell of burning filled the air and the guns continued to pound away as shrapnel clattered on to the roof and the ground.' Having survived the onslaught by the Luftwaffe's first wave, numerous bombs having exploded nearby, Bill and his parents were suddenly ordered to leave their home, the Air Raid Wardens knocking on their door to inform them that an unexploded bomb had been located in the immediate area. They were told to make their way to a Rest Centre that had been established in Keeton's Road School. Bill vividly recalled the journey that followed:

That walk was a nightmare… It was bright as day from the light of the blazing docks as we set off with neighbours, but they soon left us behind as dad could not walk quickly [due an artificial leg, the result of wounds sustained at the Battle of Loos in 1915] over the rubble and fire hoses in the streets. At South Bermondsey Station we were escorted past a UXB and as we walked along Galleywall Road with bombs whistling down and exploding nearby, people were calling us from their front door to come in and take shelter. Firemen and Wardens directed us and helped dad over obstacles, and I remember one place where a house was hit and bodies were laid out on the pavement. At Southwark Park Road, we were sent under the railway bridge and up Drummond Road and after what seemed like hours reached Keeton's Road, miraculously unscathed.

5. Quoted on www.spitalfieldslife.com.

Heinkel He 111s en route to a target in Britain during the Blitz. (National Museum of Denmark)

Above left: **The ruins of an Isolation Hospital in London after it was hit during the night raid of 20 September 1940. (Historic Military Press)**

Above right: **'Business as usual' is the message given by this shopkeeper when he opened up after a night raid by German bombers. (Historic Military Press)**

Bill has never forgotten the scene that greeted him in Keeton's Road School:

> It was chaotic with scores of displaced people arriving from all over the area, and so far as I know no proper system for logging who arrived. Many of the ground floor classrooms were full, with people and we were directed to what I think was the main assembly hall where there were no seats and only the floor to sit on… I have no idea what time it was, perhaps midnight or later as I sat tired and terrified on the floor with mum's arms around me, when a loud hissing whistling noise of a falling bomb brought a hush over everybody. I don't remember hearing the explosion, but the feeling of the blast trying to push the air out of my chest I will never forget followed by a strange sudden silence as a crushing weight fell in on me. Mum was screaming asking if I was alright and calling for dad as people around us began to call out for help and some were crying and screaming with pain and fear. I was bent double having difficulty in breathing and tried to move but we were buried in sandbags and this caused more sand and dirt to fall in on us. With mum still

crying and calling out for dad and the sounds of the agony and suffering around us, it was just too awful for words and thankfully I must have passed out.[6]

Bill came to just as rescuers were working their way through the rubble. Both he and his mother were alive, though badly shaken by the experience. Removed to a first aid station in nearby railway arches, the two were reunited with Bill's father who had been standing outside when the bomb exploded. Bowled over by the blast, he suffered nothing worse than burst eardrums and cuts and bruises.

One of the rescuers despatched to Keeton Road was a Metropolitan Police Officer, Sergeant Peters:

On reaching the building, Sergeant Peters and his men went through the playground and could see many of the classrooms were on fire. In one room they saw a fireman lying on a make-shift bedstead and his face looked as if it had been skinned. A little further along Peters and another officer were searching, by the glow of the flames, through the debris when his companion bent down and picked up what he thought was a piece of bread. To their horror, it turned out to be the remains of the limbs of a small child. Both were so disturbed by what they had found that they left the school and went back out into another part of the street. Here they discovered even more bodies lying in the footway and the road. Unable to come to terms with what had happened they stood and watched motionless for a few moments. To their relief, some of the bodies showed signs of life and it became clear that not everyone was dead.

Bill and his parents were fortunate to have suffered the blast at Keeton's Road School. A total of 31 individuals, the youngest just eight months, the oldest 76, were killed in the explosion; seven others succumbed to their wounds in the days that followed.

'Dante Had Nothing on Hitler'

Through all of this death and destruction, Ida and her mother had kept on walking. 'The streets were littered with glass, and the pavement pitted with shrapnel from a raid earlier on in the day [the 17.00 hours raid]. Far away down the Barking Road, we could see the glare of an incendiary bomb that had landed in the roadway and we decided to take to the back-streets. A pale flickering light over towards Barking turned out to be the power station which had been hit, the gas-works too.'

As they were going down one turning, an Air Raid Warden saw the two women picking their way through the debris and stopped them. He insisted that they take cover from the falling masonry and bombs and he took them into his house. There they remained until the morning:

We sat on the stairs in the dark gazing out through the open door to the street which was incessantly lit up by explosives. And how those bombs fell! Canning Town library was hit, Forest Gate got it too, and all around us seemed to be shaking. Dante had nothing on Hitler, believe me. At last, at 5 o'clock [in the morning], the all-clear went and we finally reached home to find some windows and all the ceiling down in mummy's room. Daddy was looking dreadfully drained. He had no idea what could have happened to us, and imagined the worst.

After a cup of cold milk, Ida collapsed exhausted onto her bed and quickly fell into a deep sleep. Later in the day she sat down to write a letter to a friend recounting her remarkable journey through the blitzed streets of London. 'Last night was so ghastly that I hope I never have to go through anything like it again.'

As the RAF historian Denis Richards noted after the war, in switching their bombing from the airfields to the cities, the Luftwaffe had ensured that the battle was 'now not only against the British air force but against the British people'.[7]

---

6. BBC People's War website, Article ID: A8943988.
7. Denis Richards, *Royal Air Force 1939-1945*, Vol.1 (HMSO, London, 1953), p.184.

Above left: Adapting to the circumstances forced on them by the start of the Blitz, people shelter and sleep on the platform and tracks in Aldwych Underground Station, on 8 October 1940. (Historic Military Press)

Above right: 'His head is battered and bandaged, but this Londoner is still on his feet', notes the original caption dated 23 October 1940. (Historic Military Press)

Below: Another night raid underway. Two fire-watchers are silhouetted against the glare caused by the many fires burning across London on the night of 16/17 April 1941 – the flames making it appear as though daylight had arrived hours ahead of schedule. (Historic Military Press)

Chapter 5
Destruction in the Docks

The main objectives of the first wave of German bombers on 7 September had been the capital's docks, though some of the first bombs fell on the Ford Motor works at Dagenham, followed by the Beckton gasworks in the Borough of Newham, the largest of its kind in Europe. Moments later, the bombers were over Woolwich Reach, with its three Royal Docks and their warehouses and sheds. Soon, the deadly payloads were falling among the narrow streets and crammed buildings of the East End. The crashing eruptions were followed almost instantaneously by flames as the entire docklands seemed engulfed in a raging fire.

At the West India Docks, it was the rum stored there, at the aptly named Rum Quay, that burned fiercely; at the Surrey Commercial Docks in Rotherhithe, it was the large quantities of wood. One man who recalled the effects on both locations was Commander Sir Aylmer Firebrace, the regional fire officer who was soon to become Chief of the Fire Staff. In his memoirs, he noted that 'about a million and a quarter gallons of rum were destroyed' at Rum Quay. 'Torrents of blazing spirit flowed into the dock, while burning rum puncheons exploded, flinging jets of liquid fire in all directions'.[1]

The Surrey Docks had been bombed at the same time as the West India Docks. It was there that vast stocks of soft wood, mostly imported from the Baltics, were stored. Again, Sir Aylmer Firebrace takes up the story:

Shortly after five o'clock in the afternoon, the raid warning having been received a few minutes previously, a fireman, on duty at the top of the drill tower of the nearby Pageants Wharf fire station, reported a mass of planes swarming up the river, flying low. They swooped at once for the timber – there was never any doubt as to their objective. The dock area was immediately bespattered with incendiary bombs, with here and there a few high explosives and an occasional container of fuel oil, dropped to intensify the flames. The vast area of some two hundred and fifty acres, containing thousands of standards of timber, including a lot of pitch pine and other resinous woods stored in sheds and on open ground, burst into flame. Incendiary bombs ignited the built-up deck cargoes of the many ships in the docks… They lodged, burning, in inaccessible places in the huge piles of timber stacked twenty feet high; they fired the carpet of tindery wood chips, which had accumulated on the timber storage foundations, so spreading the fire with the rapidity of flashing gunpowder. In a very short time, the heat was so intense that even the wood paving blocks in the roads were burning. Tempestuous roaring sea of fire, increasing in violence every minute, stormed its way into the heavens. The Fire Officer, faced with this inferno and waiting impatiently for bulk reinforcements, may be excused a lapse from standard phraseology when he sent an exasperated message: 'Send all the bloody pumps you've got; the whole bloody world's on fire!' As far as could be seen, it was.

Firemen drenched the timber stacks with water, but, the moment they moved their jets to a new area, the soused wood steamed, dried, and once more burst into flame. Four auxiliary fire stations were engulfed and obliterated. Pumps became surrounded by fire and had to be abandoned, their crews only just making their escape in time. On the riverbank, people were in imminent danger of being driven into the water by the flames, and had to be evacuated by boat. Those cut off by fire at South Wharf, which lies to the East of the dock area, sought refuge in a barge; with difficulty it was towed to safety by a fire boat, nosing its nightmare way between groups of small craft, most of them alight, and some burning furiously.

Forty-two huge fires were now raging; one was being fought with three hundred pumps and another required one hundred and thirty. Reinforcements poured in, some eventually coming from as far afield as Birmingham and Bristol… Of the million and a half tons of soft wood timber concentrated in the Surrey Commercial Docks, four-fifths was destroyed. Daylight… was to reveal a smoking wilderness huge

---

1. Commander Sir Aylmer Firebrace, *Fire Service Memories* (Andrew Melrose, London, 1946), p.167–9.

Above: This picture, taken from one of the German raiders on 7 September 1940, shows 'the effects of a concentrated attack on London's docks and industry districts... Factories and storehouses were seriously damaged.' (Historic Military Press)

Below left: One of many fires started in the Surrey Commercial Docks in Rotherhithe on 7 September 1940. Covering some 27 acres, the Surrey Docks were the centre of the timber import trade, so the fires that were started here developed into a single huge conflagration or fire storm. Faced with this nightmarish situation, Station Officer Gerry Knight, the fire officer in charge, sent the following, now famous, message to his control: 'Send all the bloody pumps you've got; the whole bloody world's on fire!' (Historic Military Press)

Below right: A page from the issue of the *Berliner Illustrirte Zeitung* of 19 September 1940. It shows the aftermath of the Luftwaffe raids on London at the very start of the Blitz. (Historic Military Press)

warehouses stood gutted; ships, which only a few hours previously had been discharging their cargoes, now lay, some on fire, some torn by blast, some sunk with only parts of their funnels and superstructure showing above the water. The enemy had certainly done their work with thoroughness.

It was not just the Surrey Docks and West India Docks that were hit that night. Firebrace added:

The fires in the facility of the Royal Albert and King George V Docks were an awe-inspiring sight. The situation was completely out of hand. Superstructures of ships were blazing; acres of warehouses were on fire from end to end; molten tar was flowing alight over many of the roads, often filling bomb craters with liquid fire. It was a scene of weird and brilliant devilry. Many people had to be evacuated by water from their homes in the Silvertown area, driven out by the dense fumes of burning tar products.

Reinforcements

Peter Blackmore was a successful playwright who had become a volunteer fireman after encountering a 'Join the AFS' poster in the London Underground. As the German bombers began their work on the afternoon of 7 September, he was at his station wondering what to make of the 'ominous red glow in the sky, which, had it not been in the east, could have passed for an indifferent sunset', when a colleague came in to inform that the docks were being attacked.

Not long after, Blackmore and his colleagues found themselves heading eastwards as part of the urgently requested reinforcements. As they approached the docks, they joined 'an endless queue of appliances, all steadily moving and being detailed to their exact positions.' He continues:

Bombs were falling fast and heavy. We did a great deal of ducking... and my heart was in my mouth. The journey towards a blitz, like most apprehension, can be the worst part of it... Eventually we came to a standstill at the Wharf where we were to spend the endless night. Everything seemed to be on fire in every direction, even some barrage balloons in the sky were exploding. The cinder-laden smoke which drifted all around made us think of the destruction of Pompeii.[2]

An AFS fireman from Shoreditch, L F Bastin, was among the hundreds of fire personnel who worked tirelessly from the moment that the first bombs fell. 'I saw hundreds of firemen working with bombs dropping all round', he recalled. 'On the dockside itself, right among the heart of those fires, civilians were standing round helping. Young girls and old men formed human chains passing buckets of water to the firemen when we could not get water from the hydrant... I saw great lorries burning up like matches. The fire-boats came up and helped.'

Shortly after midnight, Bastin sustained an ankle injury. Refusing to leave his colleagues, he battled on until ordered to get medical treatment. At the first aid post, he encountered five other firemen. 'One man', he remarked, 'had taken cover in a doorway when he heard a bomb whistling. His face was covered with splinters from the wood blocks in the road. He never murmured.'[3]

Such was the scale of the fires, that at one point an unbroken wall of flame stretched along the south bank of the Thames for 1,000 yards. Some of the London fire boats that had been sent to deal with the aftermath of the attack on the Thameshaven facilities were ordered back upriver to join the fray. One of the boats' captains later recalled the journey:

We kept close formation until we reached Woolwich, and then we saw an extraordinary spectacle. There was nothing but fire ahead, apparently stretching right across the river and burning on both its banks. We seemed to be entering a full of fire – no break in it anywhere. All the usual landmarks were obliterated by walls of

---

2. Juliet Gardiner, *The Blitz: The British Under Attack* (Harper Press, London, 2010), p.11.
3. 'I Was There', *War Illustrated*, No.55, Volume 3, 20 September 1940.

Above: Fire boats battle a major blaze in warehouses on the banks of the River Thames. (Library of Congress)

Left: This image shows the devastation wrought on London's docks during the attacks of 7 September 1940 – burnt out warehouses and stores, battered quaysides, and damaged merchant ships. The poor quality of this image is due to the fact that it is an example of a 'Wirephoto', when images were sent, in this case to the US for immediate publication, by telegraph or telephone. (Historic Military Press)

flame. Burning barges drifted past. For many hours, no contact with the shore was possible. We did what we could where we could as we slowly worked our way upriver.

At one time, we were just getting into position to fight a fire in a large warehouse when the whole of the riverside front collapsed into the water with a mighty splash. The contents of the building, bags of beans, pouring into the river made a sound like a tropical rainstorm. Soon after, we were surprised to see two firemen and three firewomen picking their way along the shore in the direction of Southwark Bridge; they told us they had been cut off in a control room for several hours.

South Wharf Hospital

Just being in the vicinity of the various docks in London meant that a building or individual was truly on the front line that night. This was very much the case for the staff and patients of the South Wharf Hospital, which was located along the north side of Surrey Docks. Opened in 1883 as a smallpox receiving centre, over the years the site had expanded to include facilities for the treatment and observation of patients, as well as accommodation for the staff. There was also a pier that stretched out into the Thames. The hospital's Medical Superintendent, M Mitman, later penned a report describing some of the dramatic events that night:

High explosive and incendiary bombs fell in large numbers all around the Wharf, and in a short time fires were raging. The wax-paper mills to the north, the timber yard and flats to the south, and buildings to the west were alight. Sparks began to set the nurses' home alight and the staff, consisting of the Sister-in-Charge [Sister A E Hope], 2 other members of the nursing staff, 5 domestics and 3 male staff worked hard to keep these down until the water supply inside the Wharf failed. General Mechanic W. Petley was particularly active and turned off the gas service. Meanwhile, incendiary bombs had fallen on to buildings within the Wharf. A. and C. shelters, a coke dump and trees were burning, and the fires were spreading to other buildings. The pier was alight in several places, as were barges and barge moorings in the river to the east of the Wharf. There were, thus, fires inside the Wharf and all around.

The Fire Brigade had meanwhile been removing local residents, chiefly women, old men, and a man on a stretcher, to a boat moored to the pontoon. General Mechanic W. Petley reported to the Sister-in-Charge that the Fire Brigade had ordered the Wharf to be evacuated, and that their only chance of escape was by the river. The tide was going out, the pier was alight, and petrol was stored on the pontoon. The Fire Brigade were therefore anxious that they should leave at once.

All the female staff, except Sister Hope, ran down the burning pier, 264 feet long, to the boat alongside the pontoon. Before Sister Hope could follow, another incendiary bomb fell on the pier and it collapsed. The staff in the boat were taken across to Millwall on the north side of the river, where kindly people took them into their homes and gave them tea. They spent the night in public shelters… Meanwhile, Sister Hope, left at the pier head, took shelter with Stoker W.H. Hobbs in a corrugated iron shed. Shortly afterwards firemen came to take them out. They were led between burning wards and trees to the road outside. Hope stated that she wouldn't have attempted to get past if the firemen hadn't come. She was put into a fire trailer.

Bombs were still falling, and in the middle of the night the fire brigade decided to evacuate because of the presence of an unexploded bomb. The trailer, the driven through the darkness and smoke fell into a crater in the middle of the road. The crater was full of water and Sister Hope to be lifted out by the firemen. She was taken in a car to Cherry Garden Fire Station [in Cherry Garden Street, Bermondsey] and kept there the night. Next morning, after the 'All Clear' was sounded, she was taken to Paradise Road Police Station, and after a long and roundabout journey she reached Joyce Green [Hospital at Dartford] at 3.15 p.m. on Sunday, 8th September. Sister Hope, in reporting the fire, praised the behaviour of the staff and the fine work of the men (particularly Petley, who never ceased working throughout the afternoon and night). She was particularly grateful to the Fire Brigade, to whom she undoubtedly owed her life.

Stoker W.H. Hobbs, a sufferer from asthma, who lives in one of the cottages and came into the Wharf when the trouble started, was taken to hospital next day and remained there for a month suffering from the

Left: Two pensioners washing salvaged crockery after the Royal Hospital, a home for old soldiers in the Chelsea district, was damaged by a night raid on London. (Historic Military Press)

Below: Winston Churchill visited the East End on the afternoon of 8 September 1940, to see for himself the effects of the bombing the previous night. One of the first places he was taken to was an air raid shelter that had received a direct hit, some 40 occupants being killed in the explosion. The Prime Minister is pictured here with West Ham Town Clerk Charles E Cranfield, on the corner of Winchester Street and Factory Road, inspecting the still smouldering ruin of the Silvertown Rubber Company. (Historic Military Press)

Above: A scene of devastation in the Docklands area of London, this time following a Luftwaffe attack on 17 September 1940. (Historic Military Press)

Right: The seat of Britain's government after an attack in the first few raids of the Blitz. The original caption, dated 16 September 1940, states that this picture shows 'a room attached to the House of Lords which was wrecked when an oil bomb crashed through the roof'. (Historic Military Press)

The Blitz in built-up areas such as the East End had unintended consequences, in that, later in the war, the bomb sites would provide excellent urban warfare training grounds for Allied troops. Here, a group of US Rangers are being briefed in a part of the East End prior to 'practicing house-to-house fighting' in a 'realistic city battleground in a bombed-out area of London', 8 October 1942. (Historic Military Press)

effects of the smoke to his chest. General Porter G. Edwards (a one-armed man) suffered from a burn on the nose. The following buildings were completely destroyed: Medical Officers' quarters, all wards (i.e. Shelters, A. B. C. and D.), the receiving rooms, male staff quarters, stores, boatshed, engineer's and carpenter's shops, greenhouse, No.5 cottage and their contents. Minor damage was done to other buildings. The pier was destroyed also.[4]

As so many ordinary men and women had witnessed that night, it had been a truly apocalyptic scene in and around London's docks, as the late Dr Alfred Price once described:

> There were pepper fires, loading the surrounding air heavily with stinging particles, so that when the firemen took a deep breath it felt like burning fire itself. There were rum fires, with torrents of blazing liquid pouring from the warehouse doors and barrels exploding like bombs themselves. There was a paint fire, another cascade of white-hot flame… A rubber fire gave forth clouds of smoke so asphyxiating that it could only be fought from a distance.[5]

The fire in the Quebec Yard of the Surrey Commercial Docks is reputedly the most intense single fire ever experienced in the United Kingdom.

---

4. The National Archives, HO 250/8.
5. Alfred Price, *Blitz on Britain: The Bomber Attacks on the United Kingdom* (Sutton Publishing, Stroud, 2000), p.92.

Chapter 6
Flight from the East End

As the sun came up on the morning of Sunday, 8 September, the remaining population of the East End of London, although many did not realise it at the time, had survived the most devastating bombing attack of the war to date. In terms of aerial attacks on London, the first wave of German bombers the previous afternoon had set a benchmark that would not be supplanted; never again would enemy aircraft deliver such a high concentration of bombs into a comparatively small target area in such a short period of time. Although on many occasions the Germans dropped more bombs and caused more casualties, they never again achieved the same local intensity.[1]

When the last of the bombers turned for home on the morning of the 8th, some 436 men, women and children lay dead, whilst a further 1,600 had been severely wounded. 'To try and put the first major raid on the capital into perspective', wrote Ian Jones MBE, 'more tonnes of bombs and incendiaries were dropped on London on that day than in all the First World War attacks put together. There are various estimates of the tonnage of bombs dropped in the Great War; they range from a minimum of 290 tonnes to a maximum of 368 tonnes of bombs. In just forty-five minutes on 7 September 1940, some 348 bombers dropped more than that on the East End. In twelve hours, the figure had almost doubled when, under the cover of darkness, a further 330 tonnes of bombs and nearly 16,000 incendiaries were delivered into the carnage below.'[2]

Destruction All Around

Between them, the day and night attacks had resulted in nine conflagrations (huge spreading areas of fire), 19 fires that would normally have called for 30 pumps or more, 40 ten-pump fires, and nearly 1,000 lesser blazes.[3] Large numbers of houses, factories and other buildings had been destroyed or damaged.

When the second 'All Clear' sounded at 05.00 hours on the 8th, one of the saddest Sundays London had known, people, with groans of relief, began to stretch their cramped limbs and shuffle towards the exits of their air raid shelters. Though the flames had added further horror to the devilish scenes of the night, the cold light of day brought with it a chilling reality. 'As soon as the first people get outside the shelter, there are screams of horror at the sight of the damage… smashed windows and roofs everywhere… One man throws a fit; another is sick.'[4]

Another Londoner, Lilian Burnett, recalled the widespread destruction: 'We took a walk round the houses. It was as though there had been an earthquake. Beds were hanging from bedroom floors, broken glass, bricks, rubble and thick dust everywhere. There was a funny sort of quietness, almost as though you were in another world. Not quite real.'[5]

For a number of different reasons – such as a fear of the bombers' return or the fact that they had little option, their homes and possessions all lost – some residents of the East End decided to head out of the city as quickly as they could. As soon as war had been declared a year earlier, the first evacuation of children, the elderly and the disabled had begun. It was expected that London would be a target of the Germans, and though the raid had come as a terrible shock to the Londoners, it was hardly a surprise. So, when the 'All Clear' sounded on the Sunday morning, so began the exodus from the East End.

---

1. Ian Jones MBE, op cit, p.180.
2. ibid.
3 Anon, *Front Line 1940-41* (HMSO, London, 1942), p.12.
4. Stansky, p.50.
5. Lilian Burnett, quoted in Pam Schweitzer (Ed), *Londoners Remember Living through the Blitz* (Age Exchange Reminiscence Group, London, 1991), p.27.

Above: Children from an East End London borough, made homeless by the bombing in early September 1940, pictured outside the wreckage of what was their home. (Library of Congress)

Left: With their homes destroyed, these Londoners are pictured salvaging their possessions that had survived the German bombing. (Library of Congress)

Bombed-out and homeless London residents are provided with free meals in the days after the start of the Blitz in September 1940. (National Museum of Denmark)

The Exodus Begins

A special news bulletin on Sunday morning portrayed the events of the previous day in dramatic words: 'Thousands of refugees from the smitten quarters were bombed as they fled. Mothers lay protectively over their children in the gutters under the glow of the fires as the Nazi bombers rained down death. Firefighters worked through hell. All those sights of pitiful Spain, China, Finland are left behind compared with this tragedy of London.'[6]

Some made their way to the West End, which, because it lacked the docks and industrial premises of the East End, was considered to be safer. In Richmond, hundreds of refugees had arrived by 12 September, as the *Richmond and Twickenham Times* reported: 'A thousand men, women and children arrived, after a four-hour journey down river by barge or in pleasure launches. The first relay arrived at about 12 o'clock; a later party were landing just as an air raid warning sounded and so had to take shelter under the arches by the riverside immediately, and the last 600 arrived so late that they could not be billeted… but had to spend the night at the cinema sleeping on the chairs or the floor.'[7]

Some of the evacuees headed even further west, to towns and cities such as Reading, Windsor and Oxford, all of whom suddenly found themselves dealing with a sizable influx of helpless refugees. The novelist Vera Brittain visited Oxford in the days after the opening of the Blitz, and 'found babies' nappies drying in the august Tom Quad of Christ Church; the colleges acted for a while as clearing houses while the authorities found billets for the refugees'.

6. Colin Perry, *Boy in the Blitz* (Sutton Publishing, Stroud, 2004), pp.110–15.
7. Quoted from Simon Fowler, *Richmond at War 1939-1945 (Richmond Local History Society, 2015).*

For nearly two months, between 500 and 1,000 evacuees were provided with emergency shelter in the Majestic cinema on Oxford's outskirts. Located in the Botley district to the west of the city, the cinema was an imposing building that had seating for 1,900 people in its main auditorium, as well as a café and dance hall. It was abruptly closed on 11 September 1940, right in the middle of a showing of the film *Babes in Arms* staring Judy Garland and Mickey Rooney, having been requisitioned by the government to house some of the London refugees.

It was, however, a far from satisfactory arrangement, as Vera Brittain discovered:

Covering the floor beneath the upturned velveteen seats of the cinema chairs, disorderly piles of mattresses, pillows, rugs and cushions indicate the 'pitches' staked out by each evacuated family. Many of the women, too dispirited to move, still lie wearily on the floor with their children beside them in the foetid air, though the hour is eleven a.m. and a warm sun is shining chiefly on the city streets. Between the mattresses and cushions, the customary collection of soiled newspapers and ancient apple cores is contributing noticeably to the odoriferous atmosphere.[8]

Others headed for the Essex countryside, a reported 5,000 trekking into Epping Forest, where special camps were set up for them, or the hop fields of Kent, where traditionally large numbers of Cockneys spent working holidays and from where a number of people had only recently returned. With its area almost entirely within the wider urbanised area of London, and mostly within the ceremonial county of Greater London, the County of Middlesex was, unsurprisingly, a destination of choice for many of the evacuees.

On 21 September 1940, the *Middlesex County Times* wrote:

For the second time within four months, shelter is being provided for people who have lost their homes in the course of the war. Empty houses which were prepared for the Belgian refugees in May are now being used to accommodate families from the East End of London who have been rendered homeless as a result of the air raids… One town has already received 2,500 evacuees, including approximately 1,500 who do not come under the official evacuation scheme of the East End authorities.

They have drifted into the town at all hours of the day and night, and many of them have been found at midnight and in the early hours of the morning by the wardens in the air raid shelters. Some have managed to bring small bundles of personal belongings, but the majority have nothing but the clothes they are wearing.

Various churches have lent their halls to provide temporary shelter for the evacuees. The clergy, with their wives and church-helpers, are working day and night to feed these people and to make them as comfortable as possible until more permanent billets can be found. Many of them have been working for 18 hours at a stretch… The halls are stocked with supplies of tinned meat, soups, tea, sugar, milk and bread provided by the Public Assistance Committee. When the evacuees arrive, they are taken to these halls and given a meal. Before leaving for their new homes, the Public Assistance Board provides them with sufficient money to enable them to buy their own food.

Wherever possible families are billeted together. Small families of three or four are billeted on householders, and larger families of nine, ten, eleven, twelve and fifteen are billeted in empty houses. Blankets, mattresses, etc., have been supplied by the British Red Cross and St John Ambulance Brigade, who are working in conjunction with the Women's Voluntary Services and the local clergy. Empty houses are inspected by members of the Women's Voluntary Services, who decide what furniture and cooking utensils are required and arrange for transport. Billeting officers, assisted by their volunteer staff and members of the W.V.S. co-operate in settling the evacuees in their new homes.

As the author Angus Calder once wrote, 'the homeless and the fearful trekked out in the mornings, pushing their chattels in prams or handcarts'. The Deputy Chief Air Raid Warden of Poplar, which had endured some of the heaviest of the bombing, watched the crowds amble out of the area: 'Pony carts, hand-drawn barrows, perambulators and cycles with heavily-laden carriers, all rolled out of the borough in a steady stream.'[9]

---

8. Vera Brittain, *England's Hour* (Macmillan, London, 1941), pp.215–6.
9. Constantine FitzGibbon, *The Blitz* (Faber and Faber, London, 2011), p.63.

Above left: A group of East End residents making the most of their impromptu and temporary residence in the assembly hall of a school in Essex in the days after being bombed out of their homes. The original caption states that, 'There is a new army forming in London. It is an army of civilians made homeless by unrelenting German bombing. It is a pathetic army composed mostly of women and children who are forced to seek shelter where they may.' (Historic Military Press)

Above right: For three hours on the Monday following the start of the Blitz – the 9th – King George VI, accompanied by the Queen, toured the east and southeast boroughs of London. (Historic Military Press)

The majority, though, had to stay, their jobs tying them to the metropolis. So many of those who remained in the city had become homeless, quite literally, overnight, and the homelessness of the large numbers of the working population of London would prove one of the greatest challenges of the Blitz in the months that followed.

For good reason, 7 September 1940 will always be known to Londoners as 'Black Saturday'. To the capital's residents, this first experience of a heavy air raid and the scenes of destruction, fires and mayhem were both frightening and exciting. But the one question that was on everyone's mind on the morning of 8 September was whether the raid was a one-off action by Hitler to demonstrate what he could do to Britain if Churchill did not seek some form of rapprochement or was it the start of something terrible.

In the next few days, or possibly in the next few hours, the men and women of the nation's capital would have their answer.

Residents of Lambeth who have evacuated from London in the face of the German bombing and taken up residence in caves at Dover. (Historic Military Press)

Chapter 7
Saving St Paul's

It was, of course, expected that Hitler's bombers would target some of the nation's most important structures. As a result, Walter Robert Matthews, the Dean of St Paul's from 1934, had put into place measures to fight any fires that might engulf the cathedral. One of the steps taken was re-formation of the St Paul's Fire Watch – the decision being made at a meeting of the Cathedral's management on 29 April 1939. Mr Godfrey Allen, the Cathedral Surveyor, was appointed to command the Watch and preparations were made to put the Cathedral onto a war footing.

The Watch, originally instigated in World War One and disbanded after the Armistice, called upon the experience of many who had served in its ranks in that conflict. It was quickly established that the Watch's initial strength of 62, all of whom were drawn from the Cathedral's staff, was insufficient to maintain shifts operating 24 hours a day, seven days a week. An appeal was therefore made to the wider public:

> St. Paul's Cathedral is in urgent need of double the present number of Firewatchers… The average strength at the moment is about 20 men a night. Dr. W.R. Matthews, the Dean, is sending out an appeal for volunteers and his first letters have gone to the Royal Institute of British Architects and to the High Commissioners for each of the dominions. He stated yesterday that the work is interesting, and volunteers have the unique privilege of being given the freedom of the Cathedral. They are expected to watch one night a week; but the hours of duty can be adjusted to suit individual requirements. The watchers are required to be at the Cathedral not later than 9.30 PM. Subsistence allowance is paid and bunks, blankets and mess room accommodation are provided.[1]

The appeal was successful, and, at its peak, the Watch could muster a total of 300 volunteers, 40 of whom guarded the cathedral each night. The Watch was fully activated on 25 September 1940.

The construction of St Paul's does not lend itself easily to fire defence. Mary Prendergast, who joined the Watch in 1939, remembered the problems of patrolling 'such an enormous building, with many complex avenues on the

roof; corners and crannies – there could be an incendiary bomb anywhere in a small crevice, or under some masonry. If this was not promptly removed, it could… [cause] a fire well into the building.'

Even the Dean himself appreciated the difficult task his volunteers faced:

A view of the devastation around St Paul's Cathedral as it appeared on 5 March 1941. Note what appears to be a war artist at work in the foreground, just left of centre. (Historic Military Press)

---

1. A full account of the Watch can be seen at: www.alondoninheritance.com/thebombedcity/the-st-pauls-watch/.

They were expected, if necessary, to walk along the slender beams of the Dome to reach their bombs or to thrust the nozzles of their stirrup pumps into the heart of an incipient fire. The Dome was not a healthy place in the height of a blitz and the patrol was changed at half-hourly intervals. Men have told me of the awesome feeling they experienced when carrying out their patrols in the darkness of the Dome while the battle raged around them and of how the din seemed to be magnified by the Dome like the beating of a drum.[2]

An Unexploded Bomb

With the firefighters drilled and the wardens prepared, the Watch stood ready, and St Paul's braced itself for the anticipated onslaught. It was an onslaught which, as might been expected, came on the very day of the Blitz, though, fortunately, on that first mass raid no bombs fell on or very near the cathedral.

Then, five days later, at 02.25 hours on the morning of Thursday, 12 September 1940, a Sprengbombe Cylindrich (SC) 1000 bomb fell close to the steps below the southwest tower and slammed into the roadway of Dean's Yard. This 1,000kg air-dropped general-purpose demolition bomb had enough destructive power to demolish the whole façade of the cathedral – but it failed to explode.

Hitting the pavement in front of the clock tower on the southwest of the cathedral, the bomb had penetrated the ground on a curving path, coming to rest some 15ft below street level. Since it had not detonated, there was a suspicion it might be a time fuse. It was duly labelled a Category 'A' unexploded bomb – it must be neutralised before it exploded, whatever the cost.

This task was passed to Temporary Lieutenant Robert Davies, the Commanding Officer of 16/17 Section of No 5 Bomb Disposal Company Royal Engineers. Based at Bunhill Row in the City of London, where the Honourable Artillery Company also had its headquarters, Davies, at nearly 40 years of age, was the third-in-command of the capital's bomb disposal resources.

When he arrived outside St Paul's, Davies found that a wide space in front of the steps had been cordoned off by the police and traffic had been stopped from using Ludgate Hill. The cathedral stood quiet in its enforced silent setting. For the first time in centuries, the daily service went unperformed.

Though at this point Davies did not know which type of bomb lay in the crater, its angle of descent indicated that it was close to the foundations of the cathedral and that it was near the entire trunk telephone network to the north of England. If the bomb was fitted with a Type 17 series long-delay fuse, then it had a maximum delay of about 80 hours.

By the time that Davies began his investigation, 12 hours had already passed. Speed was therefore of great importance if St Paul's was to be saved.

The six sappers with Davies jumped into the crater and began to remove the rubble that had fallen in on top of the bomb. Almost immediately, the men collapsed unconscious. The bomb had fractured a 6in gas main, and the soldiers had been overcome by the fumes in the crater. A repair team from the Gas Light and Coke Company was working nearby and

Members of the Watch making their way up the stairs of the Whispering Gallery in St Paul's on the 16 February 1940. (Historic Military Press)

2. M J Gaskin, *Blitz, The Story of 29th December 1940* (Faber and Faber, London, 2005), p.69.

they came to the assistance of the sappers. The soldiers were taken to hospital, though they soon recovered and returned to help Davies.

The gas workers cut off the mains supply, but not before a fire broke out and the fire brigade had to flood the main pipe with water. Most of the day had passed before the sappers could recommence digging. Time was slipping away.

The bomb disposal team continued digging throughout the night, but soon after dawn on Friday, three of the men were burned when a spark accidentally ignited another gas leak. Everyone threw themselves to the ground – except Davies, who stood seemingly unruffled on the rim of the crater. The casualties were treated at nearby St Bartholomew's Hospital and once again were back at work that same day.

At last, when they had dug down about 12ft, the sappers located the bomb. A hawser was passed round it, but as the men tried to dig the bomb free, it slipped from the thick rope and slid even further down. It slithered another 12½ft down into the ground. There was simply nothing for it but for the men to keep on digging.

A Race with Death

Davies and his team dug on, with no sleep and barely a break, down through the London clay, their endeavours punctuated by the occasional dash for cover when further bombs fell close by. They worked on throughout Saturday.

A Mr Frisby acted as a go-between the sappers and the Dean, providing 'frequent reports of hope and despair, ranging from "up in the afternoon", or "a couple of hours" then "before dark". He explained the special difficulties being encountered by a bomb settling down in the soft sub-soil. As fast as the squad dug, the bomb penetrated further by its own weight.'

All through Saturday night they dug and on into Sunday morning, knowing, as they did that 'the building represented a symbol of survival and freedom for Britain'.[3] Almost 80 hours had elapsed; at any minute, the huge bomb might detonate. As the *Daily Mail* put it: 'These most gallant – yet most matter-of-fact – men of the RE are many a time running a race with Death.'

At last, at a depth of 27½ft, Sapper George Wylie touched metal – they had located the bomb again. Davies examined the bomb and found that it was indeed fitted with a Type 17 long-delay fuse protected by a ZusZ 40 anti-withdrawal device. This type of device had been identified just ten days earlier on a bomb that had dropped on Swansea. No remedy had yet been devised to deal with this new threat, and so the instructions that had been issued were for all of these bombs to be destroyed in situ. This was simply not an option for Davies. Somehow, he would have to remove the bomb intact without disturbing it to the extent that it would detonate.

Davies ordered the streets to be cleared from St Paul's to Hackney, where unexploded bombs were being taken for safe disposal well away from any houses at what became known as the 'bomb cemetery' on Hackney Marshes. Sapper Wylie and his section gently eased a half-inch thick wire rope round the bomb, the other end of which went through pulleys attached to a lorry.

Slowly, they winched the bomb from the ground, but the strain proved too much, and the line snapped. Undaunted, the sappers cautiously repeated the operation, only for the wire to give way yet again.[4]

By this time, it was almost midday, and everyone was becoming extremely nervous. The bomb had long passed its 'safe' time. In what was described as 'in almost frantic haste', another lorry was paired in tandem with the first. The wires were reattached and together the two vehicles pulled the huge bomb clear of the clinging clay. It was tightly lashed to a cradle and gently placed onto the flat bed of an awaiting Army lorry.

'These men went about their grim task with complete sang-froid', the Dean had noticed. 'They showed some signs of excitement, however, when, their work completed, Mr Frisby entertained and thanked them in the local hostelry!'

Davies dismissed his men to save them from any further danger. Then, preceded by police motorcycles, he drove 4½ miles through the empty streets of east London, which had been cleared of people by the police,

---

3. John Frayn Turner, *Awards of the George Cross* (Pen & Sword, Barnsley, 2006), p.11.
4. The Very Reverend W R Matthews, *Saint Paul's Cathedral in Wartime 1939-1945* (Hutchinson & Co, London, 1946), p.37.

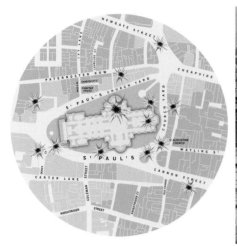 

Above left: **A map showing the location where the main high explosive bombs fell in the precincts of St Paul's Cathedral during the Blitz. The unexploded bomb that fell on 12 September 1940 is that by the very bottom left corner of the cathedral, just to the right of the top of Dean's Court. The buildings in the green shaded portions of the map were generally still standing at the end of the Blitz, whereas the brown coloured areas denote mostly open spaces where every building of note had been destroyed by bombs and fire. It is impossible to indicate where the many thousands of incendiary bombs fell on and around the cathedral. (Historic Military Press)**

Above right: **A retouched wartime press image of workmen repairing the bomb-damaged roof of St Paul's Cathedral on 31 October 1940. (Historic Military Press)**

to Hackney Marshes. The bomb was unloaded and exploded in a controlled detonation. The resulting crater was more than 100ft wide and 8ft deep.

The news of Lieutenant Davies' and Sapper Wylie's exploits soon hit the headlines. 'It seems though they are trying to make me a national hero', Davies wrote to his wife, 'but I don't take any notice of it. I am still the same old dad.'[5] Sapper E J Norman viewed the operation with that same sang-froid the Dean had witnessed: 'Scared? Well, we just dig it up as if digging the garden and we take no more notice of a bomb than if it were a worm.'[6]

The saving of the cathedral lifted the morale of the Londoners who had endured night after night of punishing air raids. 'London is wild with praise for them', wrote one woman. *The Times* considered it to be the most 'outstanding deed of heroism so far recorded in the capital'. A service of thanksgiving was held in the cathedral.

The Bombs Strike

Early in the morning of 10 October 1940, the Germans scored a direct hit on the cathedral when a bomb struck the roof of the choir, bringing down tons of masonry. After crashing through the lead and timber roof, the SC 500 bomb (half the size of the 12 September bomb) exploded on one of the stones of the transverse arch nearest the apse – believed to have been the actual keystone – some 60ft from the extreme east end wall of the cathedral. The main force of the explosion was borne by the roof and vaulting of the choir, and the roof was lifted from end to end by the blast. The falling masonry completely destroyed the High Altar. Fortunately, the floor held up as the Archdeacon of London was sleeping just underneath the spot on which the masonry fell.

---

5. M J Jappy, *Danger UXB: The Remarkable Story of the Disposal of Unexploded Bombs during the Second World War* (Chanel 4 Books, London, 2003), pp.55-6.
6. James Owen, *Danger UXB: The Heroic Story of the WWII Bomb Disposal Teams* (Little, Brown, London, 2010), p.119-21.

Above left: Bomb-damaged buildings are demolished in Ludgate Hill following the raid of 10/11 May 1941. On the left is the spire of St Martin-within-Ludgate Church, with, a short distance beyond, the western façade of St Paul's Cathedral. (Historic Military Press)

Above middle: Damage to the High Altar in St Paul's Cathedral that resulted from the bomb that struck early in the morning of 10 October 1940. (Historic Military Press)

Above right: An evocative view of St Paul's Cathedral among the smouldering ruins of surrounding bomb-damaged buildings during the Blitz. (Historic Military Press)

Wren's magnificent old building looked terribly scarred yet, as the American journalist Ernie Pyle recorded, it still inspired the Londoners: 'They go and look at it without sadness and they say, "We would rather have it that way in a free London than have it whole like Notre Dame in an imprisoned Paris."'[7]

The worst of all the raids to affect the cathedral, however, was on 29 December 1940. That night, 28 incendiary bombs fell on or near the cathedral. This time, it was the members of the Watch and the fire brigade that saved St Paul's. At about 21.00 hours, one of the incendiaries actually penetrated the outer shell of the dome and the lead began to melt. Luckily, it burnt its way through the roof and fell onto the Stone Gallery where it was easily extinguished.

Watching from some distance away, Edward R Murrow, the well-known American correspondent, saw the fire. He duly announced on air, that 'the church that means most to Londoners is gone. St Paul's Cathedral... is burning to the ground'.

Fireman Sam Chauveau was on duty that night: 'By the time we finished tackling the fires on the roof of the [Stock] Exchange, the sky, which was ebony black when we first got up there, was now changing to a yellowy orange colour. It looked like there was an enormous circle of fire, including St Paul's churchyard.'[8]

The fires were raging to the south and east of St Paul's, running along Cheapside and Cannon Street. An even greater conflagration was north of the cathedral, covering most of the northwest of the City and up into Finsbury, Islington and beyond. The fires were spreading to within a matter of yards from the north and south sides of the cathedral and threatening to become one unstoppable blaze.

---

7. Gaskin, op cit, p.73.
8. See www.bbc.co.uk/news/magazine-12016916.

Above: **The view through the hole in the floor of the North Transept into the crypt below after the attack in April 1941. (Historic Military Press)**

Right: **An aerial view of the devastation around St Paul's Cathedral during the German bombing of London in the Blitz. (Historic Military Press)**

It certainly seemed that the cathedral was doomed, especially as the Thames was at low tide and the water-mains had been broken. But tanks, baths and pails had been filled with water and placed around the building just in case such an eventuality occurred.

At the fire brigade headquarters in Lambeth the telephone rang. One firewoman who saw her officer take the call noticed him turn white. 'That was the Prime Minister', he told her. 'He told me that St Paul's must be saved at all costs'. The message was passed onto City Control and relayed to the Watch.

So, with nothing more than stirrup pumps, buckets and sandbags, they fought the fire in small mobile teams that tackled each fire separately. The Chapter House on the north side was destroyed and so was the whole area around Paternoster Square. But the cathedral itself stood, as Dean Matthews observed, 'conspicuous and isolated among the ruins' around.[9]

The Fire Raid

The eight-hour raid that was made against the capital on the night between 16/17 April 1941, by a force of some 450 bombers, produced the highest number of individual fires that ever occurred in the London Region in one single night. Of these, some 1,500 were in the London County Council's area, including 400 that were classified as 'serious', and which, in theory, would have required a response by more than ten pumps.

In this onslaught, St Paul's was hit by a 500lb high explosive bomb and a 'heavy shower' of incendiaries. Once again, it was the volunteers of the Watch that found themselves on the forefront of the battle to save the cathedral. Commander Firebrace later expressed his admiration for these 'stout-hearted local defenders'. 'Without their constant watch and ward', he concluded, 'the cathedral – a most difficult building to safeguard – must have been destroyed'.

'Save St Paul's' had been Churchill's plea and, on several occasions, the men of Bomb Disposal, the Watch and the fire brigade did just that.

---

9. Ann Saunders, *St Paul's: The Story of the Cathedral* (Collins & Brown, London, 2001), p.178.

Chapter 8
Blitz Gallantry

That Lieutenant Robert Davies, Sapper George Wylie and their colleagues had saved St Paul's was beyond dispute; nor was the clamour in the press for official recognition of their actions. The Ministry of Home Security had, for example, placed on record the statement that 'only the courage of the officer, his NCOs, and the men prevented St Paul's being levelled to the ground'.

It was against this backdrop that King George VI felt it appropriate to award both men the new George Cross – the citations for which were published in a supplement to *The London Gazette* of 27 September 1940. It had been just three days earlier that the George Cross, which soon became known affectionately as the 'Civilian VC', had been instituted.

In announcing the new award, the King said: 'In order that they should be worthily and promptly recognised, I have decided to create, at once, a new mark of honour for men and women in all walks of civilian life. I propose to give my name to this distinction, which will consist of the George Cross, which will rank next to the Victoria Cross.'[1]

Though its Royal Warrant would not be published in *The London Gazette* until 31 January 1941, its wording included the following: 'It is ordained that the Cross shall be awarded only for acts of the greatest heroism or of the most conspicuous courage in circumstances of extreme danger.'

Until 1940, the Victoria Cross was the highest award that could be granted for acts of courage, but this was available only to members of the armed forces. The Empire Gallantry Medal was open to civilians, but it ranked lower than the Victoria Cross, as did the Albert Medal and the Edward Medal.

It was the changed nature of warfare in the first 12 months of World War Two that brought about the need for a civilian gallantry medal that would have a comparable status to that of the Victoria Cross. The Blitz had brought warfare from the battlefields to the UK's cities and the towns. Now the home front could be as dangerous as the front line, and where there is danger there is often self-sacrifice and heroism.

King George VI added that, 'The Cross is intended primarily for civilians and award in our military services is to be confined to actions for which purely military honours are not normally granted'.

At the same as the introduction of the George Cross, a Royal Warrant revoked the Empire Gallantry Medal. All living recipients or the next-of-kin of those who were deceased were instructed to exchange their medals for a George Cross. Thirty years later, in 1971, the surviving recipients of the Albert Medal and the Edward Medal were also invited to exchange their award for the George Cross. A total of 112 Empire Gallantry Medal holders, 65 Albert medallists and 68 Edward medallists made the exchange.

Davies and Wylie were the first two servicemen to receive this award. As the man who commanded the removal of the bomb and who had taken sole charge of its transportation, Davies was an obvious candidate for the George Cross. For his part, the citation for Wylie's award explained that 'The actual discovery and removal fell to him. Sapper Wylie's untiring energy, courage, and disregard for danger were an outstanding example to his comrades.' It is worth noting that for their involvement in the dramatic events at St Paul's and in the subsequent removal of the bomb, Sergeant James Wilson and Lance-Corporal Herbert Leigh were awarded the British Empire Medal.

Despite the fact that it was intended to be the 'Civilian VC', 76 of the first 100 awards of the George Cross were to members of the armed forces, predominantly, as in the case of Davies and Wylie, for their bomb

---

1. Kevin Brazier, *The Complete George Cross* (Pen & Sword, Barnsley, 2012), p.1.

Above: **One of the saviours of St Paul's Cathedral, Sapper George 'Jock' Wylie, who was, along with Lieutenant Robert Davies, awarded the George Cross for his actions. (Historic Military Press)**

Above middle and above right: **The front and reverse of the George Cross. A plain cross with four almost equal limbs, 48mm in height and 45mm wide, the medal is suspended from a suspension bar decorated with laurel wreaths. (Historic Military Press)**

Right: **Second Lieutenant Wallace Lancelot Andrews, 22/23 Bomb Disposal Section, depicted during the action for which he was awarded the Empire Gallantry Medal, later exchanged for the George Cross. An unexploded bomb had fallen at Crohamhurst Golf Course, near Croydon, Surrey, on 26 August 1940. The fuse fitted was needed for evaluation, and despite the dangers, Andrews made repeated attempts to recover it. Not succeeding, it was blown up. (Historic Military Press)**

disposal work. However, the very first person to be directly awarded the GC, as distinct from those who received theirs by exchange, was a civilian – and a remarkably courageous one too.

Bridlington Under Attack

Thomas Hopper Alderson had been serving as a part-time Detachment Leader in the ARP Rescue Parties in Bridlington. When the bombers arrived in his part of Yorkshire on 15 August 1940, the 37-year-old was soon in action when a pair of semi-detached houses, among other buildings, was destroyed. The falling masonry trapped one woman alive. Thomas Alderson tunnelled under the unsafe brickwork and rescued the lady.

Above: The damage caused to the Woolworth's store in Prince Street, Bridlington, during an air raid on 23 August 1940 – a scene that was again attended by Thomas Alderson and his team. (Courtesy of Fred Walkington MBE)

Left: A portrait of Thomas Alderson GC in Civil Defence uniform, wearing both his George Cross and Silver Issue RSPCA Gallantry Medal. (Courtesy of Mrs J P Wilson)

Some days later, on 21 August, two five-storey buildings were demolished by bombs, the debris penetrating into a cellar, trapping 11 people. One section of the cellar had completely given way, actually burying six of those trapped under heavy debris. Once again, Alderson tunnelled to rescue the trapped people. He struggled on for 3½ hours, tunnelling 13ft under the main heap of wreckage with his bare hands. In a BBC radio interview conducted in October 1940, Alderson describes the events that day:

We were called out and found a heap of ruins. The flames were still about and bombs were clomping [dropping] in the distance. We searched around and found a basement door partly uncovered. One of the house walls was still standing and it didn't look very safe, but we started at that basement door. We cleared it: nothing is too small to move, and I passed bits of brick and plaster and wood back along the chain of men 'til I managed to get inside. The ground-floor joists had collapsed: they were jammed between the basement wall and floor, and this had given protection to four people in a corner. There was a big farmhouse table in the middle of the floor: this had partly collapsed and was half-supporting the beams and smashed walls from the floors above. Lying on my side, I began to work a hole over the table keeping a wary eye on the unsafe debris, and then passing bricks and rubbish back along the chain of men. At last, there was enough space for us to slide the four people headfirst into the hole over the table, swing their legs 'round and then pull them backwards through the basement door.

However, Alderson and his team became aware that a boy and girl were also still trapped under heavy joists towards the centre of the basement.

The [farmhouse] table had now to be carefully broken up and removed, and again debris was passed out bit by bit. There wasn't room to use standard ARP jacks. I called for motorcar jacks and with these managed to raise the main joist a little 'til it started to crack. By jacking immediately underneath the crack, I raised the joist still further. By this time, the cellar was filling with coal gas and water appeared to be rising on the floor. The boy and girl were in severe pain, so I called in a doctor to give them an injection. We had to work them free from the joist and slide them out but at last, after four hours' work, with hand torches as our only means of light, it was done. Planes were still humming about overhead, but I had been too busy to notice them.[2]

---

2. Quoted by Lord Ashcroft KCMG, PC, in 'Hero of the Month', *Britain at War* Magazine, June 2013.

On a third occasion, five people were again trapped in a cellar, and once more Thomas Alderson went to their rescue. He crawled, clambered, crouched and dug away under the ruins of the building for hours with a three-storey-high wall tottering above him. When Alderson reached the trapped people, two were still alive and these were brought to the surface, though one later died.

Alderson's award of the George Cross was gazetted in the same supplement of *The London Gazette* as those of Davies and Wylie, though he was listed first. His citation described his actions as being of 'sustained gallantry, enterprise and devotion to duty during enemy air raids'. His citation ended with the following: 'By his courage and devotion to duty without the slightest regard for his own safety, he set a fine example to the members of his Rescue Party, and their teamwork is worthy of the highest praise.'

The first formal investitures of the George Cross took place at Buckingham Palace on 24 May 1941. As he presented Alderson with his award, the King remarked: 'You are the first recipient of the George Cross. It gives me very great pleasure to hand it to you.'[3]

'Great Bravery and Endurance'

At the height of the Blitz, it might have seemed that the George Cross was being earned, if not yet awarded, almost every day. One such example is provided by the actions of 30-year-old Auxiliary Fireman Harry Errington. Serving in the AFS, and attached to a fire station on Shaftesbury Avenue, Errington and two colleagues, John Hollingshead and John Terry, were resting in the basement of what had been a garage pre-war, when the building received a direct hit just before midnight on 17 September 1940. All of the floors caved in, and about 20 people, including six firemen, were killed. His citation for the George Cross noted the following:

> Errington and two other Auxiliary Firemen were the only occupants of the basement of the building at the time of the explosion. The blast blew Errington across the basement, but although dazed and injured he made his way to the other two Auxiliaries, whom he found to be pinned down, flat on their backs, by debris. A fierce fire broke out, and the trapped men were in imminent danger of being burnt to death. The heat of the fire was so intense that Errington had to protect himself with a blanket. After working with his bare hands for some minutes he managed to release the injured men and dragged them from under the wreckage and away from the fire. While he was so engaged, burning debris was falling into the basement and there was considerable danger of a further collapse of the building. He carried one of the men up a narrow stone staircase partially choked with debris, into the courtyard, made his way through an adjoining building and thence into the street. Despite the appalling conditions and although burned and injured, Errington returned and brought out the second man. Both Errington's comrades were severely burned but survived. He showed great bravery and endurance in effecting the rescues, at the risk of his own life.

The kind of actions for which civil defence personnel were recognised. The original caption, dated 21 October 1940, states: 'After toiling ceaselessly for 15 and a half hours, rescue squads succeeded in extricating alive this aged man who was buried by debris when a bomb dropped by German night raiders wrecked a building in the London area. The man, about 70, can be seen in the hole as rescuers strive to free him.' (Historic Military Press)

3. Kevin Brazier, op cit, p.2.

Errington was invested with the George Cross by King George VI during a ceremony at Buckingham Palace on 21 October 1941. It is perhaps somewhat surprising, given the events which are detailed on the pages either side of this chapter, that Errington was the only member of the London AFS, and one of just three firemen in total to be awarded the George Cross during World War Two.

'For Wider Distribution'

As with military operations, the Honours and Awards Committees had a number of options open to them when considering how to recognise an individual's bravery. By way of an example, if you take the fierce bombing and firestorm that enveloped London on 29 December 1940, events that night resulted in a total of 44 gallantry awards – more than for any other single event during the Blitz. These comprised a single MBE, 22 British Empire Medals, 13 Commendations for Brave Conduct, and eight George Medals.[4]

Instituted at the same time as the George Cross, the latter was another new award that resulted from the developing war on the Home Front. King George VI himself noted that it was intended 'for wider distribution' than the more senior George Cross. It was to be awarded to civilians for acts of great bravery, but not so outstanding as to merit consideration for the George Cross. The Royal Warrant added that the 'award in our military services is to be confined to actions for which purely military honours are not normally granted'.

The first awards of the George Medals were announced in the same supplement to *The London Gazette* of 27 September 1940. In total, 14 George Medals were awarded in respect of seven separate incidents, all of which were related to attacks by the Luftwaffe.

An example of the military recipients of the George Medal is Second Lieutenant Frank Robert Martin. Serving in 12 Bomb Disposal Company RE, the 29-year-old's citation provides the following account:

> [He] was informed that an unexploded bomb had fallen on a private residence where a lady was lying dangerously ill and could not be removed. He had recently lost four of his men in dealing with a similar bomb and decided to recover this one by himself, so as not to risk any further lives. After several hours of solitary excavation, he succeeded in extracting the fuse (which he found to be still ticking) and removed the bomb. It is considered that Second-Lieutenant Martin's action undoubtedly saved the lady's life at the imminent risk of his own.

Second Lieutenant Martin lost his life a few weeks later when a bomb he was working on exploded on 22 October 1940.

Claiming to be 16 years old, Charity Anne Bick lied about her age to enlist as an ARP messenger in West Bromwich – she was, it is said, only 14. It was during a raid on West Bromwich that she undertook her gallant actions:

> During a very heavy air raid, Miss Bick played an heroic part under nerve-racking conditions. At the outset when incendiary bombs began to fall she assisted her father, a Post Warden, to put out one of these, in the roof of a shop, with the aid of a stirrup pump and bucket of water. The pump proved to be out of order, but, nothing daunted she proceeded to splash the water with her hands and eventually put out the fire. While endeavouring to get out of the roof, the charred rafters gave way and she fell through to the room below and sustained minor injuries.

Despite her injuries, Bick continued in her duties, making repeated journeys between her post and the Control Room, a distance of approximately 1¼ miles, during the height of the raid.

Miss Bick is variously described as the youngest ever George Medal recipient or the youngest female recipient. In either case, she is a worthy example of the very people that King George VI had in mind when he introduced his new gallantry awards in the face of the Luftwaffe's campaign against Britain's towns and cities.

---

4. For more information see: https://www.nickmetcalfe.co.uk/gallantry-during-the-blitz

Above left: The headstone that marks the last resting place of Second Lieutenant Frank Robert Martin, 12 Bomb Disposal Company RE, who was killed, aged 29, on 22 October 1940. Martin had previously been awarded the George Medal for his bomb disposal work. (James Luto Collection)

Above middle and above right: A G VI R issue of the George Medal. (Historic Military Press)

Below: A Royal Engineers Bomb Disposal unit at work on an unexploded 1,000lb bomb in the grounds of the German Hospital, Dalston, during September 1940. (Historic Military Press)

Chapter 9

Blitzed Britain

To the utter dismay of Londoners, the German bombers returned on 8 September and, indeed, every day thereafter for some considerable time. But, on 5 October, after suffering heavy losses and with the onset of autumn bringing the promise of longer nights, the Luftwaffe's daytime attacks pretty well ceased. With neither the RAF nor London knocked out, and Hitler having postponed plans for an invasion (indefinitely as it turned out), for the rest of October the Luftwaffe started to despatch such aircraft as could be spared from its battle of attrition against Britain's capital on the longer-term mission of striking at industry. This policy became even more pronounced in November.

Front Line 1940-1941 noted:

The character of raiding changed, and attacks on the provincial cities moved from the margin to the centre of the picture. London had failed to yield quick results; and the German Air Force, well exercised over the Thames, was becoming proficient enough in the once despised art of night bombing to undertake attacks on smaller and more elusive targets than the sprawling capital. There was to be no knock-out blow – that was clear. But the enemy may have still thought it possible to achieve the same ultimate result, given time, by striking intermittently at industrial centres and ports.

The Front Widens

So, in the weeks and months that followed, Göring's bombers ranged far and wide across the United Kingdom. These new tactics, targeting the nation's industrial centres and port cities, were inaugurated by the infamous raid on Coventry on the night of 14 November 1940. London would still suffer – indeed its worst nights were still to come – but the burden of the war on the Home Front would no longer be borne by its citizens alone.

As the official account went on to state:

No provincial target had to endure anything like the long-drawn-out continuity of the first three months' nightly attacks on London. None of them suffered a comparable sum total of damage. Parliament has been told that in the London Civil Defence Region twice as many houses were made inhabitable by air attack up to the middle of 1941 as in the whole of the rest of the country. This make's London's ratio of destruction, in proportion to the population, eight times as great as that of the balance of the country. The death rate from air attack throughout the period of the raids was several times greater in a collection of the hardest hit London boroughs than in heavily raided provincial cities of similar population. About half of the country's total of deaths and serious injuries occurred in London.

One of the many night raiders, what appears to be the fuselage of a Junker Ju 88, that never returned. (Historic Military Press)

A few of Plymouth's residents make their way through streets that have been completely decimated by the Luftwaffe's bombing. (Historic Military Press)

All things considered, as the Blitz unfolded, few could claim that it was anything other than an attack on the whole country. Very few areas were left untouched by air raids. 'In one after another of the target cities', concluded *Front Line 1940-1941*, 'the whole centre was wiped out, either in one night or by the accumulation of bombs. and fire spread over several raids.' The account continued:

> True, in Southampton, though whirlwinds flung away the shops of the long High Street, the Bargate still stood, defying bombs as it had defied the centuries. But in Portsmouth, the bright shopping centre of Southsea was gone. In Liverpool the great homes of the shipping companies were hollow shells. In Manchester, one side of Piccadilly stood like the ruins of Ypres. Hull is scarred from side to side and end to end. In Swansea, Bristol, Plymouth, a large part of the centre of the town is now a levelled expanse of soil pitted with broken brick and scored here and there with the remains of walls.

Birmingham
Britain's third most-bombed city after London and Liverpool

Four nights after the Coventry attack, the Luftwaffe selected England's second largest city – Birmingham – for destruction. The city had already suffered ten lesser raids, and nearly 400 of its citizens had lost their lives so far. But, on 19 November 1940 came its first major attack, with more than 800 'incidents' in that single night. The Germans dropped more than 400 tons of high explosive bombs, and one of the city's most important factories, the Birmingham Small Arms (BSA) works, was hit and 53 workers were killed.

Three nights later the Germans came again, but in smaller numbers. It was still enough to start hundreds of fires and kill a large number of civilians, including many of those in the civil defence services.

The most prolonged raid of the entire Blitz followed on 11 December. For 13 hours, Birmingham was pounded by 278 bombers, which dropped some 25,000 incendiaries. There were more than 1,000 incidents and the pressure on the emergency services was so great that first aid parties helped rescue people from the rubble

Bomb damage in James Street, Aston Newtown, Birmingham, after the raids of 1940. Note the twisted remains of several Anderson shelter. (via Historic Military Press)

of their homes and factories and the rescue men were seen treating casualties. Birmingham was the home to many medium-sized metal industries, all of which had been adapted to war production. These factories and workshops were scattered among houses and behind stores around the city. Often, therefore, when a factory was hit so were the houses of the workers.

Win Dunn was just 13 years old when the war came to Birmingham:

I remember watching Marks and Spencer's and the market hall burning in a reflection in my bedroom window in the company of my mother. One high explosive bomb just missed my house and hit a nearby petrol station, leaving a great big crater where it used to be. It was so near we were lucky to have escaped with our lives. Ours was the only building left standing in the street… The injured were brought into our house and the family helped dress their wounds.[1]

A total of 263 people were killed and 243 badly injured during that never-to-be-forgotten night.

The Germans, inevitably, were far from finished with Birmingham. Raids continued throughout the rest of the year and into 1941. On the nights of 9 and 10 April, the city was subjected to two heavy raids. In the first of these, 235 bombers dropped 280 tonnes of explosives and 40,000 incendiaries, demolishing much of the city centre; the following night, it was the outlying towns which were attacked. These two raids caused 1,121 casualties. The last raid of the Blitz on Birmingham was on 16 May.

Southampton
Site of a Supermarine Spitfire factory

As well as being a major port, Southampton was home to a Supermarine factory, building Spitfires, in the suburb of Woolston. At the same time, being on the South Coast, it was within easy reach of the German bombers. Little wonder then, that Southampton was the subject of 57 attacks during the war.

The first of those raids came in September 1940, the Supermarine factory and the city itself being hit. But the Blitz really began for Southampton on 6 November, with the German bombers targeting the city centre. One bomber dropped its payload on the city's Art Gallery and an art block where classes were in progress. Thirty-five people were killed, including 15 young students.

This, though, was a relatively minor assault (only 12 bombs were dropped) compared with what followed 17 days later, on 23 November. That time, 60 enemy bombers appeared over the city. Doreen Marjorie Bennett and her family took to their garden shelter: 'For the whole night, wave after wave of bombers came over, systematically destroying the whole of the town. Incendiary bombs followed, and the whole sky was alight with a vast blaze stretching over many miles. Firefighters drained the ponds on the nearby common when the water supply gave out, until there was no more water.'[2]

1. Win Dunn, BBC People's War website Article A2842599.
2. BBC People's War website, Article A3271042.

Severe though this raid most certainly was, a far greater attack was delivered across two nights, those of the weekend of Saturday, 30 November and Sunday, 1 December, which involved 200 enemy aircraft. The first of these lasted for six hours, turning the city into 'a blazing inferno in which every living thing seemed doomed to perish'. The docks were hit, and a large part of the wharves and sheds were left in a state of 'tangled chaos'.

The attack killed 137 people as approximately 800 high explosive bombs and 9,000 incendiaries rained down on Southampton. Ninety-six died as they took cover in shelters when bombs ripped through the roofs. Some 1,169 homes were also destroyed, and landmark premises such as the Ordnance Survey Office, the Echo building and the General Motors factory were also wrecked.

Some of the fires that started on that awful Saturday night were still blazing when the bombers returned on the Sunday night. Such was the level of destruction, the *Portsmouth Echo* declared that the attack had left the city a 'charred and blackened' ruin.

For Southampton, the worst was over, the city being subject only to two more large scale attacks which were comparatively far less deadly. Those apart, only the occasional sporadic attack from lone aircraft troubled the city.

Bristol
The fifth most heavily bombed British city

Another port, that of Bristol, suffered its first attack the night after that of Southampton, on 24 November. The raid started when pathfinder flares began illuminating the city at 18.50 hours. After the flares had marked the target, the following waves of aircraft dropped high explosive bombs with the intention of, among other things, shattering the city's water mains and diminishing the Fire Service's capacity to act. Lastly, there were the aircraft dropping incendiary bombs. It was the fires generated by the incendiaries that did so much to tear the heart out of Bristol that night, for within an hour more than 70 fires were raging across the city and by 20.00 hours the Germans had succeeded in severing the water mains and the firemen were forced to relay water from the river and harbour.

According to the German crews of Luftflotte 3, on their return, the results were akin to those achieved at Coventry. Whole blocks of buildings were reportedly on fire – one jet of flame reportedly rose for nearly 400 metres into the night sky, producing a fire that reached was visible from 250km away. Some 1,540 tons of high explosives and 12,500 incendiaries fell on Bristol that night.

The concentration point of the German attack was on the built-up areas on both sides of the city centre docks with the intention of eliminating Bristol as an importing port supplying much of the material for the factories of the Midlands and the south of England. In this respect, the raid was not a great success. It was true that the city itself suffered severely, as did parts of the suburbs and some important war-production factories – the Bristol Aeroplane Company factory made Blenheim and Beaufort bombers and the Beaufighter – but the docks themselves escaped with surprisingly light damage.

Winston Churchill tours a bomb-damaged area of Bristol during the Blitz. (Historic Military Press)

A Bristol woman wrote the following in her diary for 24/25 November: 'We've been through hell. Never have I experienced anything like it… Fires and bombs everywhere. We went to the cellar but couldn't settle down, so went to the sitting-room. We didn't need any light for the room was lit up with the glare of the fires.'[3]

Yet there would be more to come. Between that night and 11 April 1941, there were five more major bombing raids on Bristol and other minor ones. But it was the night of 24 November 1940, that saw the worst destruction wrought on the city by those 148 German raiders. It was of those five or six hours of horror that, in 1942, The Lord Mayor, Alderman Thomas Underwood, wrote: 'The City of Churches had in one night become the city of ruins.'

Liverpool
Along with the rest of Merseyside, Liverpool was the most bombed area outside of London in 1940

The Liverpool–Birkenhead conurbation had come under attack on ten occasions during 1940, particularly on 28 November. Then came a period of calm lasting through the first ten weeks of 1941, when the Luftwaffe concentrated its attention against other targets. For Liverpudlians and those living in the nearby areas, that respite came to an abrupt end on the evening of 12 March 1941, when they suffered the heaviest attack of all.

That night, the raiders found clear skies over the target, and with the aid of a near-full moon they had little difficulty in identifying their objectives. In an effort to draw part of the attack away from the main target, 'Starfish' decoy sites were lit in the open country around Liverpool. But this stratagem deflected few raiders from their objectives. The vanguard of the raiding force attacked from altitudes of between 16,000ft and 19,000ft using the Y-beam bombing system and dropped large numbers of incendiary bombs to mark the target area.

The defences, such as the barrage balloons, could do little to minimise the destruction as Luftflotte 3's after-action report on the night's attack stated:

> Extensive fires were started in the dock area and parts of Birkenhead adjoining it. Three burning ships were observed in the harbour. There were numerous clusters of fires scattered over the target area. In Birkenhead there were three large fires, of which two were in the dock area. There was a medium-sized fire in the north-eastern part of Birkenhead, East Float, and a medium-sized fire in Birkenhead cattle dock. At 2335 hours there was an explosion with a high jet of flame.

This jet of flame was almost certainly one of the gas holders at Wallasey, both of which were destroyed.

The British account of the raid agreed with many aspects of the raiders' descriptions of events, save in one important aspect: the weight of the attack fell on Birkenhead and Wallasey to the west of the Mersey estuary, rather than Liverpool itself to the east of the estuary. An estimated 270 groups of incendiary bombs fell on the built-up area. These started more than 500 fires, of which nine reached major proportions. About 400 high explosive bombs detonated, causing widespread damage. During the attack, and a smaller one on the following night, a total of 631 people were killed, and a similar number injured.

The onslaught was far from over. In the first eight days of May 1941, for example, Merseyside was bombed almost every night. In all, 1,900 people were killed, 1,450 seriously wounded and 70,000 made homeless. In Bootle, 8,000 out of 17,000 houses were destroyed or damaged during the Blitz.

Sheffield
A major centre for armaments manufacture

Sheffield, long known for its steel mills and arms and munitions factories, escaped the attentions of the Luftwaffe until 12 December 1940. When the sirens sounded at 19.00 hours, as they had done many times before, life in the Yorkshire city continued as normal – until a shower of incendiaries began to drop.

---

3. Angus Calder, *The People's War, Britain 1939-1945* (Panther, London, 1971), p.238.

This communal grave in Sheffield's City Road Cemetery marks the last resting place of 134 victims of the bombing of Sheffield in December 1940. (Historic Military Press)

The main intention of the German attack was to destroy the factories along the Don Valley, but the first wave of Heinkels encountered low cloud in the target area and possibly mistook a road called the Moor, which ran through the south of the city centre, for Attercliffe Road, which was the major arterial road through the industrial belt. By the time that bombers carrying high explosives came on the scene at about 21.00 hours, the fires that marked their target were centred in the heart of the city.

For nine hours on that moonlit winter's night, the bombers droned overhead, unleashing death and destruction on its crowded buildings and untried people. As fire and the subsequent damage spread among the commercial buildings in the city centre, one basement shelter after another became untenable. In one main street alone, 2,000 people had to be moved through a double line of fires to safer refuges.

As the hours went by and the bombs kept falling, communications across the city were disrupted, rendering organised help and rescue almost impossible. First aiders wandered through the rubble-strewn streets on foot, carrying their first aid kits in their hands, and stopping when they saw persons in need. Ambulance men also had to take to their feet, in their case it was not equipment they had to carry, but the stretchers of the wounded.

The morning of the 13th revealed a scene of almost total ruin. One of the most disturbing sites was that of the London Mart Hotel, popularly known as the 'Marples'. Instead of the familiar landmark, there now stood a pile of masonry 15ft high. The cellar of the building where many had sought sanctuary had collapsed, and the civil defence teams considered that no one inside could possibly be left alive

The rescue teams turned their attention elsewhere until, at 10.00 hours, it was discovered that seven men had miraculously survived, and by the middle of the afternoon all were recovered. Just how many died in that basement has never been determined. The bodies of 64 people were recovered, as well as the partial remains of six or seven others. Only 46 were identified.

The Germans returned just one more time to Sheffield, three nights later. The two raids resulted in approximately 300 enemy aircraft bringing death to more than 660 people and injury to 1,500 more. Around 40,000 were made homeless.

Manchester
Suffered what is often called 'The Christmas Blitz'

Though the city's first attacks had been back in August 1940, the heaviest raids on Manchester took place on two consecutive nights, those of 22/23 and 23/24 December 1940. Unsurprisingly, the pair have come to be referred to as 'The Christmas Blitz'.

It was shortly after dusk on 22 December that the bright white light of flares lit the sky above the city from end to end. It is said that the Luftwaffe crews were guided to their target in part by the fires still burning in Liverpool from the attack there two days earlier – worse still, many of Manchester's firemen and ARP personnel had not yet returned from Merseyside.

As more bombers arrived over Manchester, the sky's colour changed from white to red, as the incendiaries took hold, and the low clouds reflected the crimson of growing fires in the city centre and at Stretford with its Trafford Park industrial area. The latter had been turned over entirely to war production.

A firefighter or civil defence worker can only stand and watch as a building is engulfed in flames during 'The Christmas Blitz' in December 1940. (via Historic Military Press)

Kathleen Fox was a volunteer nurse in the St John's Ambulance Brigade, and when the raid began, she ran to the first aid post through Old Trafford's Seymour Park with incendiaries falling all around her: 'The noise of exploding bombs, chains of shells from our guns exploding in the sky, the terrifying screams of bombs falling made my dash to a shelter a journey of complete horror. Manchester was a raging inferno, encircled by a wall of fire, the sky for miles illuminated… What a terrible night.'

It was Stretford that was the focus of the second German raid the following night, though many streets in the city centre were blocked by debris, and hundreds of fires raged through the poorer part of Manchester, whipped up by strong winds. 'There were big fires everywhere', wrote journalist Cyril Dunn, 'the air stank of smoke and the streets were full of black ash as if there'd been a volcanic eruption. The destruction was enormous & spectacular… the whole of the Royal Exchange [was] gutted & burning, whacking great buildings blasted into ruin, water spurting into the road from burst mains, the cathedral; shattered glass everywhere like dirty drifts of pack ice.'

The Christmas of 1940 was a cold and bleak one for the thousands of Mancunians who lost their homes. The same for the families of the 684 who were killed, or the 2,000 who were injured.

In a further raid on the industrial complex of Trafford Park on 11 March 1941, a bomb hit Manchester United's famous Old Trafford football stadium. The pitch was torn up and the stands demolished. It was not until four years after the war that the team was able to return.

Cardiff
The Luftwaffe attacked one of the biggest coal ports in the world

It was not just English ports and cities that became the targets of the German bombers. For Wales, its first major night of terror was 2 January 1941, when an estimated 125 aircraft attacked Cardiff, with the city's docks as their main objective. It was a cold, clear night with near perfect visibility. Despite this, it was not the docks which suffered the worst of the widespread destruction.

One reason for this was the use of large-scale decoy fires code-named 'Starfish'. These were sites constructed a few miles from the city or town they were to protect. They consisted of elaborate light arrays and fires, controlled from a nearby bunker and laid out to simulate a fire-bombed town. It has been estimated that 102 high explosive bombs fell on the decoy site to the southwest of Cardiff, which would otherwise have added to the devastation that was wrought on the Welsh capital that night.

Even so, with 14,000 incendiaries being dropped on Cardiff, the city was badly hit. A vast sheet of flames could be seen from miles away, and a rubber works, a paint factory and transport offices were hit, and railways were put out of action. One of the city's most historic buildings, Llandaff Cathedral, was damaged by a parachute mine, creating, 'a scene of utter desolation… stout oaken doors were split like matchwood and torn from their hinges… the floor was cluttered with fallen timber and broken slates'. The top of the spire collapsed into the church yard and tombstones were propelled through the air, landing as far as half a mile away. Of all the British cathedrals, only that in Coventry suffered worse damage during the Blitz.

Above left: **The high altar of St David's Cathedral in Cardiff after the bombing in 1941. (Historic Military Press)**

Above right: **An example of the assistance that was provided to those communities that suffered heavily during the Blitz – in this case a mobile laundry operated by the Women's Voluntary Service pictured in May 1941. (Historic Military Press)**

Most parts of the city were hit to a fairly even degree, and, as well as industrial premises and churches, other public buildings suffered damage to a greater or lesser degree. In terms of residential property, almost 700 building were either completely destroyed or rendered uninhabitable.

One heart-warming tale was recounted by rescue workers who set off amid the terror and confusion of the raid to see if anyone could be saved from the rubble of a demolished house. As they surveyed the debris, they heard the notes of 'God Save the King' drift up through the pile of masonry. After digging through the rubble, the rescuers found a six-year-old-boy who had found refuge under a staircase. He had been trapped there for six hours, lustily singing the national anthem at the top of his voice for much of the time. When asked by his rescuers why he had kept singing for so long, he answered: 'My father was a collier and he always said that when the men were caught and buried underground they would keep singing and singing and they were always got out.'

Portsmouth
The home of the Royal Navy attacked

Portsmouth suffered its first raid on the night of 10/11 January 1941, in which a staggering 40,000 incendiaries were dropped. The bombers approached Portsmouth from the direction of Le Havre, Dieppe and Cherbourg at a little after 18.35 hours. Of the 180 enemy aircraft that took to the sky that night, 155 were despatched towards Portsmouth.

The first phase of the attack lasted until 21.00 hours, by which time the glow of the fires was visible from the French coast. Bombing was reported as generally being very accurate, illuminating the city for the second wave which arrived over Portsmouth at 23.37 hours. One witness recalled that 'was like a great firework display', the sky 'blood red and streaked with the silver of searchlights and gunfire'. Much of the latter came from warships in the harbour and naval base.

As the home of the Royal Navy, citizens of Portsmouth knew that their city was certain to be on the German target list and had prepared accordingly. A total of 25,000 Anderson Shelters had been supplied by the government, of which 14,000 were erected on behalf of householders by the Portsmouth City Engineers. In addition, there were 123 semi-underground trench shelters built as well as more substantial brick shelters. Tunnels cut into Portsdown Hill were also used. The city was also heavily defended with searchlights, anti-aircraft artillery and barrage balloons.

Despite these precautions, the effects of the bombers were considerable. The Hippodrome theatre, Clarence Pier and the iconic Guildhall, among many other structures, were badly damaged. The main shopping streets such as Kings Road and much 18th and 19th-century housing were reduced to rubble.

Jean Gamble and her family were instructed to leave their house to go to a public shelter in Somers Road, in the grounds of St Peter's Church. When they arrived there, the shelter in the grounds was full, so they were sent down into the bowels of the church. 'We were lucky', wrote a relieved Jean, 'because we hadn't been in there long when there was a mighty explosion which shook the boiler room where we were. The explosion was a direct hit on the shelter in the grounds that we had tried to get to previously.'

When the 'All Clear' sounded the following morning, Jean and her family left the church: 'There was devastation all the way round, complete and utter devastation. There was no electricity, no gas, no water. It was like a scene of a movie. You would have to live through it to be able to imagine what it was like.'[4]

Swansea
Endured the 'Three Nights' Blitz'

As an important port and the site of the first oil refinery in Britain, Swansea was high on the Luftwaffe's target list. It was the subject of a raid as early as June 1940 but was visited only by single or small groups of aircraft until 1941, when Swansea endured what became known as the 'Three Nights' Blitz'.

Those three nights were 19, 20 and 21 February when the city was visited by 250 enemy aircraft. Light snow was falling on the frozen streets of Swansea that first night when, at 19.30 hours, the first bombs fell through the snowflakes. It was the start of the worst period in the city's history.

Elaine Kidwell, a civil defence volunteer, recalled the second of those dreadful nights:

That night they dropped more incendiaries and even flares which seemed to hang in the sky for a long time, lighting everything up. There were also land mines on parachutes being dropped, and they blew up every bit of glass blew out as well. There was glass everywhere, and the pavements and roads shone with

all the reflections of every piece… The hill opposite the town is called Kilvey Hill, and thousands of fire or incendiary bombs had fallen on the hill, amongst the bracken and had gone on fire. Because they were phosphorous, they burned for many hours. It lit up the town like daylight and the bombers could see the town spread out beneath them. Lots of bombs fell on the Townhill housing estate, killing a lot of people. One man told me that his young sons were killed in front of him, and he gently laid them together on his front lawn.

A German propaganda drawing depicting a Junkers Ju 88 attacking an 'industrial plant' in the UK during the Blitz. (Historic Military Press)

4. BBC People's War website, Article A2636318.

Elaine and her co-members braced themselves for the night ahead: 'The shelters were all open and the people had all moved into them long before the sirens had gone off. The Amber Alert came and went, and then the Red warning came, and we all made for our places. Running up the road we blew our whistles, and everybody took cover.'[5]

Altogether, Swansea endured 14 hours of attacks in those three nights, resulting in more than 11,000 properties being damaged or destroyed by the 1,273 high explosive bombs and the 56,000 incendiaries that were dropped on the unfortunate city. Almost 900 properties were destroyed and 11,000 damaged. In the aftermath of the bombing, the King and Queen, as well as Winston Churchill, made a point of visiting Swansea.

Clydebank
Out of a population of 50,000, 35,000 were made homeless

It was not until March 1941, that Scotland suffered its most destructive raid of the war. On the nights of 13 and 14 March, the munition-making town of Clydebank, in the industrial area of Clydeside to the west of Glasgow, was virtually wiped off the map.

It was a clear, frosty night along the Clyde when, at 21.00 hours, the sirens began their chilling wail. The first bombs shattered the town's water mains, and huge craters in the roads and the heaps of rubble created severe problems for the rescue services. The fire brigade had to run hoses all the way from the Forth and Clyde Canal, an exhausting effort.

There was little protection from the bombs, with many preferring to construct temporary little shelters in the lowest parts of their homes rather than gather in the public shelters. One such was built in the 'ladies' hallway of a tenement block, where one woman took refuge holding her sister's baby:

> We could hear bombs all around, you could see glowing red from the houses on fire. It sounded as if every bomb was coming at you, then it seemed to whoosh away and you'd hear the explosion and feel the shake. About two o'clock in the morning we heard this one come down, it was different, it seemed to take a long time, we were terrified and were praying, I lifted the lid of the coal bunker and threw the baby in, 'at least she'll be saved' I remember thinking. The bomb kept coming, then it just seemed to stop, there was a massive explosion. We were thrown all over the place by the blast, I thought we had all been killed. We couldn't breathe and the dust and dirt filled the air, doors were blown off, floors ripped up and the tenement smashed. We were trapped in the building.[6]

Though they were not dug out of the rubble until 06.00 hours, the decision to remain in the hallway of the tenement saved their lives, as the shelter in the street outside received a direct hit.

That night, 1,200 people lost their lives in Clydebank and a further 1,000 people were seriously injured, with many more hurt less severely. The destruction of the town was almost complete, with only eight out of approximately 12,000 houses left undamaged. The Scottish Regional Commissioner justifiably described the Clydebank Blitz as 'a major disaster'.

Plymouth
For size of population, Plymouth suffered the worst of all

In the early days of the war, Plymouth had considered itself safely remote from the medium-range bombers of the enemy. But, after the fall of France, the great naval port became not just an obvious target of the Luftwaffe but an accessible one.

---

5. Elaine Kidwell, BBC People's War website, Article A2922996
6. See 'The Clydebank Blitz' on tommckendrick.com.

Firemen at work, damping down the still smouldering ruins of a building in one of Plymouth's main thoroughfares following a German raid. (Historic Military Press)

From 30 June until the end of the end of the war, the city endured 59 raids, resulting in a total of 4,448 civilians being killed, wounded, or missing, believed killed. In addition, approximately 1,300 service personnel became casualties. The heaviest of the attacks, and the most deadly occurred on the successive nights of 20 and 21 March 1941, when 336 civilians were killed, followed by five terrible nights in April, which cost the lives of 590 people.

With thousands of high explosive bombs and tens of thousands of incendiaries falling on the city and the naval dockyards, the destruction during the springtime attacks was immense. There was not a single part of the city which was not touched. The shopping centres of both Plymouth and Devonport were completely wiped out. Residential property in the districts of Hoe and Northroad was severely damaged, as were hotels and clubs.

The Service establishments suffered to an equal degree. One of the most serious incidents was at the Royal Naval Barracks, where a petty officers' block was struck and severely damaged. Many of the buildings that held important maintenance and support services were hit and most of the senior officers' residential building were demolished.

Further afield, the grandstands at Plymouth Argyle's Home Park were completely destroyed, at a time when they were packed with the furniture from houses damaged in earlier attacks. Even the Milehouse bus depot could not escape the German bombs, with about 80 buses being damaged or written off.

As far as residential property was concerned, in total throughout the Blitz, Plymouth had 72,102 damaged houses and flats. This was more than the total number of houses in existence before the start of the bombing. This strange statistic suggests that a percentage of properties were damaged two or three times.

Fire was the main cause of the loss of so many buildings, estimated at around 75 per cent of the total, the city's fire appliances proving incapable of dealing with so many simultaneous outbreaks. This meant that the city's proud citizens often had to watch helplessly as Plymouth grand buildings burnt to the ground. Although cities such as Liverpool, Birmingham and London had more bombs dropped on them, when the size of the population is taken into account, it was Plymouth that suffered the worst of them all.

Belfast
Suffered the deadliest single-night attack outside London

Northern Ireland did not escape the attention of the Luftwaffe, though it was not until the later stages of the Blitz that the port and shipyards of Belfast came under attack. It was inevitable that the Germans would want to target Harland and Wolff, one of the largest shipyards in the world, as well as Short Brothers, which made the Sunderland flying boat, among the many important industrial sites in the city.

The first attack, on the night of 7/8 April, was a comparatively minor affair, but on 15 April, Easter Tuesday, 200 bombers arrived to inflict widespread damage on a city ill-prepared for such a bombardment, with the highest population density per area in the UK at the time and the lowest proportion of public air raid shelters.

One of those that had its own shelter was the Magee family. They lived on Shore Road adjacent to the railway shunting yard, which was highly likely to be a target of the enemy bombers. So they had an air raid shelter in their back yard, just big enough for young Roy and his mum and dad. When the sirens sounded, the three Magees headed for the shelter. Then they waited. 'Next came the droning of the German planes. That sound sent a chill down our spines, we knew what was coming', recalled Roy.

'Then came a huge thud like a giant fist had punched the ground. The concrete roof of the shelter lifted a few inches letting in a flash of white light, revealing the fear written across my parent's faces, then clunked back down. Then the deafening explosion itself ripped through the air. It went on and on with us not knowing if the next one would land on us.'[7]

Many Belfast families left the city for the countryside, as indeed did animals, both wild and domesticated. Roy Magee remembered that in the brief period of silence between the winding down of the sirens and the start of the bombing, the night was broken by the noise of the pounding of feet and hooves. Eventually, the Magees joined the exodus and headed out of the city.

The raid of 15 April resulted in the deaths of some 900 people, making it the deadliest single night attack upon any UK city outside London. As the fires continued to burn out of control, fire crews were sent both from the Irish Republic and from mainland Britain. On that terrible night, 50,000 houses were damaged, more than half the houses in the city, and 100,000 people were rendered homeless.

Hull
One-third of the population left the city each evening

Sitting on England's eastern shore, Hull was horribly exposed to the attentions of the Luftwaffe. The statistics of the Blitz on Hull reveal starkly the extent of the destruction the city suffered at the hands of Göring's bombers in their efforts to neutralise this important port. By the end of the war, of the 192,660 habitable houses recorded in Hull in 1939, only 5,938 escaped damage, with 152,000 people rendered homeless at one time or another. Some 3,000,000 square feet of factory space were wiped out and the docklands hit repeatedly. Half of the city's main shopping district was demolished, and 27 churches were destroyed together with 14 schools.

The first raid on Hull took place on 4 September 1940, followed by a further 19 attacks up to the end of the year. These were light in nature and gave little indication of what was to come. On the night of 13/14 March 1941, 80 planes dropped 39 tons of high explosives on the River Hull 'corridor'. The Luftwaffe returned the following night, but not in great force. Four nights later, on 18/19 March, the German bombers were back, in what was the heaviest raid Hull had so far experienced. In one tragic instance, a parachute mine scored a direct hit on a public shelter, killing many of those inside.

Deaths generally in Hull were considered to be comparatively few in number due to the provision of more than 15,000 Anderson Shelters by the local authorities, supported by large numbers of brick and concrete domestic shelters. Approximately 2,000 indoor Morrison Shelters were delivered, and 2,300 communal shelters were erected in streets and terraces for the use of residents in congested areas. Another factor that helped lessen the casualty rate was the practice of people 'trekking' into the surrounding countryside. It has been estimated that as many as one-third of the population left Hull each evening to sleep in the woods and the fields.

Early in May 1941, Hull's docks were targeted, with two major raids on consecutive nights, beginning with a six-hour onslaught on 7 May. After the second raid, on 8/9 May, the whole of Riverside Quay area was left devastated by fire. Built by the North Eastern Railway in 1907, the 2,500ft-long quay had been parallel to Albert Dock and fronted the Humber estuary. Records also show that some 450 people had been killed and ten per cent of the population made homeless.

---

7. BBC People's War website, Article A4044458

Chapter 10

Bombed Whilst on Air

'This is the BBC Home Service' was the famous introduction that heralded the start of news broadcasts and information bulletins that kept the world notified of the progress of the war.

The Home Service began broadcasting on the night of 1 September 1939. Ever since the fateful meeting between Neville Chamberlain and Adolf Hitler at Munich the previous year, the BBC had been preparing secret plans for the changes in its output in the event of war. Whatever happened, the broadcasting service had to continue.

This presented the BBC with two problems. The first was that the radio beacons could be easily detected by enemy aircraft; the second was the production of a continuous output regardless of the effects of large-scale bombing. The solution to the first problem was found by distributing BBC units around the country instead of centralising them upon London. The second was to broadcast only one of the existing eight programmes, on a choice of two wavelengths. That one programme was the Home Service.

Early on the evening of 1 September, the message was sent from Whitehall that set the BBC's war-time changes into operation. The broadcasting engineers opened their sealed orders and went into action. Within 90 minutes, the change-over had been completed, and at 20.15 hours, the Home Service went on the air for the first time.

The BBC's television service, which had been operating to a small number of people since 1936, had already closed down. At noon on 1 September, a Mickey Mouse cartoon was being shown when the television service was suddenly blacked out. Like the radio beacons, it was feared that the transmitter could

Above left: A view of BBC Broadcasting House in London during the first few months of World War Two. The building on the right is All Souls' Church in Langham Place. (National Museum of Denmark)

Above middle: A rear view of Broadcasting House showing damage caused in the air raids in World War Two. (Historic Military Press)

Above right: A view of one of the rooms in BBC's Broadcasting House in London after it had been bombed and sustained damage in the Blitz. (National Museum of Denmark)

have provided navigational aid for enemy aircraft. (That same Mickey Mouse cartoon was shown on 7 June 1946, when BBC television reopened.) Before the war, the BBC operated for 14 hours a day. With the change to one service, the hours were extended to 17.

Though there was only one radio service, its content being predominately war-related, there was quite a degree of variety in the programming. Sometimes reports were recorded live and broadcast later; these recordings were often highly dramatic, painting a vivid picture of an ensuing engagement.

On the whole, it was the BBC's natural way to record facts in an unemotional and unbiased fashion. Indeed, the bland delivery of the news bulletins angered many. As one listener complained:

The material damage is slight and casualties few! Change your record, the public is tired of it. 10/- a year [the licence fee] for a lying machine, you won't get many 10/- from Londoners for lies, lies, lies. Take a day ticket on a London tram. Listen to conversation. See how much confidence we have in the BBC. Look for your slight material damage. But, of course, you cannot see thousands of hearts broken, they are not material damage.[1]

Nevertheless, it was incumbent upon the BBC not to reveal information that might prove valuable to the enemy. Therefore, such phrases as 'Fires were started, casualties have been reported' became standard reporting terminology. Even London, amongst many others, would simply become 'a town in southern England'.

The matter-of-fact tone adopted by announcers was reflected in the dress they wore. Even though their transmissions were by radio, and obviously could not be seen by the listeners, a strict dress code was enforced – announcers had to wear evening dress. But nothing could exemplify the BBC's unruffled approach more than the dramatic events of 15 October 1940.

'Expression of Amazed Indignation'

The famous newsreader Bruce Belfrage was in a studio located in the basement of Broadcasting House reading the nine o'clock news. He had got as far as saying 'the postscript tonight' when there was the smothered, but unmistakable, sound of an explosion. At exactly 1 minute and 50 seconds past the hour, a delayed action bomb exploded.

Belfrage paused to blow dust off his script. Then the voice of Lord Lloyd of Dolobran, who was in the studio to deliver the 'postscript' could be heard off-microphone, saying, in an urgent tone, 'It's alright.'

Belfrage gave a slight cough. 'I beg your pardon', he said, and then calmly continued without a tremor – 'quickly gathering confidence', as one newspaper reported. However, as fellow newsreader Joseph Macleod later remarked, 'The expression of amazed indignation on Bruce's face was a sight to see'.

Dropped by one of the 200-strong Luftwaffe bomber force directed against London that night, the delayed-action bomb had entered Broadcasting House through the window of the room housing the telephone switchboard on the seventh floor at about 20.15 hours.

The bomb crashed through floors and walls until its passage was finally halted in the music library located two floors lower down. It was a full 15 minutes before it was found by staff. There were other bombs falling nearby at the time, and the noise and damage the bomb caused on its journey was so great that no one realised at first that it was actually a 'delayed action' device that had not yet exploded.[2]

Harold Bishop was one of the senior engineers on duty in Broadcasting House that night:

I was in the basement at the time, and I was told that there was a large bomb on the fifth floor... We all wondered what to do with this thing, and three or four of my people, in the civil engineering department actually, said they thought it might be a good idea if they got some chair legs and try to heave this bomb out of the window, which, of course, was the silliest thing ever, but they decided to try to do that.[3]

1. Quoted in Philip Ziegler, *London at War, 1939-1940* (Alfred Knopf, New York, 1995), p.123–4.
2. Antonia White, *BBC at War* (BBC, London, 1945), p.9.
3. Interview with Sir Harold Bishop, 1977, BBC Oral History Collection.

Soon after this, the unthinkable happened:

> Sad to relate, when they were doing that, it went off, about ten minutes past nine while the news was being read by Bruce Belfrage. Two or three, I can't remember which, of the people who were trying to get this wretched bomb out of the window were killed, plus a number of others on the floor below, who had been told about it and who had been told to come downstairs, but who said 'Oh no, we won't bother, we'll stay where we are'.

As Belfrage momentarily paused in his broadcast, the shock waves from the bomb's blast raced down the lift shaft and through the ventilation system, covering everything with dust. The damage was extensive. Thousands of precious gramophone records were ruined, the important news library was wrecked, and the telephone switchboard was left as a tangled web of splinters and wires.

Behind the scenes, as the building shook, there was darkness, the crash of falling masonry, choking smoke and dust. Human beings were thrown against walls or pinned under wreckage.

Two floors below the music library, Studio 3A had been bustling with staff from the BBC's Monitoring Unit. They had been busy processing the latest transcripts of foreign radio programmes sent by tele-printer from their colleagues at Wood Norton, where the actual eavesdropping was done.

Mary Lewis, who had left her post at the Duplicating Section for the night and, like Bishop, was taking shelter in the basement, recalled the rescuers who were soon desperately trying to reach those trapped in Studio 3A:

> At the time, the place seemed to rock a bit and a lot of dust came down, but nothing much happened actually in the concert hall, but then we soon realised that people were trapped in the studio on the third floor, and throughout that night you could hear drills trying to get them out… It was pretty unpleasant because nobody quite knew, I think, how many people were involved in this particular incident.[4]

Also working away in the basement of Broadcasting House was the American broadcaster and journalist Edward R Murrow. Busy writing notes in the tiny underground studio that was shared by three big US radio networks, Murrow had also heard the dull thud of the bomb exploding higher up in the building. At the same time, the window separating him from the BBC engineers in the adjacent room suddenly cracked.

As the dust was settling, the Senior Programme Assistant in charge of the BBC's output that night calmly spoke to the corporation's studio in Bristol, informing them they might have to take over broadcasting 'at any moment'. In the end, that eventuality never arrived, and BBC London kept transmitting without a break.

Whilst accepting that 'Broadcasting House was thrown into a certain amount of confusion I might say with this noise, people rushing about in all directions', he was certain what had prevented a bigger tragedy: 'The place was in a mess, but due to the extraordinary construction of Broadcasting House, with no inside well… was such that it withheld the vibrations of this 500lb bomb going off, and apart from a few floors collapsing, the main fabric of the building was not affected, which was really quite remarkable.'

---

4. Interview with Mary Lewis, 1978, BBC Oral History Collection.

Service Continues

Murrow was one of those who went on air in the hours after the explosion. Reporting to audiences in the United States, he spoke of 'friends being carried on stretchers past his door to the first aid room, and of a pervading smell of iodine'.[5] Murrow provided little other detail. The British censor who had sat with his finger poised on the cut-off switch, ready to step in should the American start to provide information that might have been of benefit to the enemy, need not have worried.

What Murrow may not have known at that point was that six members of the BBC's staff had been killed outright in the explosion. Fire-watcher Horace Parker, Sub-Editor George Sokolow, Teleprinter Operator Ada Sixsmith, Monitoring Clerks Euphemia Shearer and Cecily Noble, and Company Fireman George Robilliard never returned home from their shifts that night. A seventh person, Defence Assistant Charles Gaetjens, succumbed to his injuries the following day at the Middlesex Hospital.

Even as the broadcasters continued to reach out, undaunted, to audiences around the world, and the bodies of the casualties were removed, the clearing up began at Broadcasting House. At 06.00 hours the following morning, the news librarian was trying to salvage the remains of his precious files, carefully accumulated over many years, from a hastily arranged pile outside Broadcasting House in Portland Place. Only with great difficulty did he prevent himself being arrested by a passing policeman on suspicion of looting.

Marjorie Redman, a sub-editor on the BBC's *The Listener* magazine, recalled her arrival at work that same morning: 'There is a gaping hole in the side of the building, but except that the telephones are not working, most people are able to use their offices and get on with their jobs as usual.'[6]

The historian who wrote the official BBC wartime history in 1945 recalled how much of a serious problem the damage to the telephone exchange was:

To lose the news library was bad enough; it was like losing one's memory. To lose the switchboard was even worse; it was like being struck deaf and dumb. [Every internal] phone in the building was out of action and the small emergency switchboards which were brought into use carried only eight lines instead of the usual seventy. Working in barely tolerable conditions in the basement, with sweat pouring down their faces, the 'telephone girls' carried on dealing with calls at the rate of eight per second.

The following day, the BBC established a committee of enquiry, the intention being to see what lessons could be learnt from the incident. 'It tried hard not to point the finger of blame, and praised both the bravery of the firefighters and the initiative of a young Overseas Presentation Assistant, Mr Carse, who… had first warned the Monitoring staff of the grave danger they were in.'[7]

Dante's Inferno

Broadcasting House suffered even more damage on Sunday, 8 December 1940, when a parachute mine landed nearby in Portland Place.

A BBC employee, L D MacGregor, left Broadcasting House just after 22.45 hours that Sunday evening and had made his way to the cycle shed in Chapel Mews:

The customary nightly air raid was in progress, and, as we left the cycle shed, we could hear the distant sound of aircraft and A.A. gunfire. We were just entering Hallam Street from the Mews when I heard a shrieking, whistling noise like a large bomb falling. This noise continued for about three seconds, and then abruptly ceased as if in mid-air. There was no thud, explosion, or vibration. I particularly remember this, as I'd heard this happen once before, and was curious as to what caused it and why it stopped.[8]

5. M J Gaskin, *Blitz* (Faber and Faber, London, 2005), p.5.
6. Marjorie Redman MBE, *Consequently This Country is at War with Germany: War, Life and the BBC* (Propagator Press, Leeds, 2009), p.231.
7. See www.bbc.com/historyofthebbc.
8. R49-321, a typescript account by L D MacGregor in the BBC archives.

MacGregor returned to Broadcasting House, and soon found himself in conversation with two policemen, Police Constable (PC) Vaughan and PC Clarke, at the building's entrance. Whilst chatting, MacGregor noticed 'a large, dark, shiny object' land silently in the street nearby, followed seconds later by what he thought was a tarpaulin. He immediately voiced his concerns to the policemen.

A Defence Officer on the roof of Broadcasting House had also witnessed the parachute mine's descent. He had just enough time to make a telephone warning, watching as it drifted slowly down, before it canopy became entangled in a lamp post near to the Langham Hotel.

Having been alerted by MacGregor, the police officers started to make their way over to inspect the object when PC Vaughan, who was in front, suddenly turned and ran back shouting a warning. 'At that moment', continued MacGregor, 'there was a very loud swishing noise as if a plane were diving with engine cut off – or like a gigantic fuse burning. It lasted about 3 or 4 seconds.'

MacGregor goes on to vividly describe the moments that followed:

Before I could… lie down flat, the 'thing' in the road exploded. I had a momentary glimpse of a large ball of blinding white light and two concentric rings of colour – the inner one lavender and the outer one violet – as I ducked my head. The 'ball' seemed to be ten to twenty feet high… Several things happened simultaneously – my head was jerked back due to a heavy blow on the dome and rim of the back of my steel helmet. I do not remember this for as my head went back, I received a severe blow on my forehead and at the root of my nose. The missile bent up the front rim of my steel helmet and knocked it off my head. The explosion made an indescribable noise – something like a colossal growl – and was accompanied by a veritable tornado of air blast. I felt an excruciating pain in my ears and all sounds were replaced by a very loud singing noise (which I was told later was when I lost my hearing and had my eardrums perforated). I felt that consciousness was slipping from me.

Confused and in agony, MacGregor was far from out of danger. 'The blast seemed to come in successive waves', he added, 'accompanied by vibrations from the ground. I felt as if it were trying to "spin" me and tear me away from the kerb.'

It was at this moment that he was struck again, this time of the front of his right temple. When he was later being treated at a first aid post, the medical staff removed a 'piece of bomb' from this wound.

Broadcasting House was badly affected, with almost every window being blown out. The mine blast blew out many street-facing windows, tore through several offices and wrecked a car parked outside. Small fires were again tackled by BBC fire squads. A more serious blaze on the third floor threatened the main tower and ventilation shafts until extinguished by the AFS. The basement studios and sub-basements suffered serious flood damage from fire hoses.[9] Studio 3E was completely burnt out. The adjacent All Souls' Church and Langham Hotel both sustained damage, as did many other properties in Portland Place.

Badly wounded, MacGregor was one of more than 50 BBC staff who were injured that night, out of the 300 or so on duty. On this occasion, none of the BBC's staff were killed, though the body of 23-year-old PC John Vaughan, who had only been engaged for two months, was found on the pavement just outside Broadcasting House. The area was described by the BBC's civil engineer as 'a scene from Dante's Inferno'.

With the dislocation of services across London, the staff would often spend the night in the basement of Broadcasting House, three floors below ground for safety. 'Wandering through the basements at night you saw corridors littered with mattresses on which tired men and women were trying to snatch a few hours' sleep', recalled one employee. 'Some slept in their offices, others in rows on the floor of the concert hall.'[10]

Even the dress code for announcers was relaxed with 'jerseys and sports coats, flannel bags and shirt sleeves' replacing the hitherto mandatory black suit and black tie. (In those days, women were not allowed to read the news.)

Unlike German radio, which was often put out of action by the Allied bombing campaign, the BBC never went off air – not even when Broadcasting House itself became a victim of the Blitz.

---

9. For more information, see www.westendatwar.org.uk.
10. Antonia White, op cit.

Above left: Looking down on the ruins of another building that was damaged during the explosion of the parachute mine on 8 December 1940 – the Queen's Hall. A concert hall in Langham Place, London, the Queen's Hall first opened in 1893. This picture of the interior was taken later in the war, after the hall was completely destroyed in the devastating air raid on London during the night of 10/11 May 1941. Both Broadcasting House and All Souls' can be seen in the background. (National Museum of Denmark)

Above right: Another famous London landmark after the passage of German bombers. This image of bomb-damaged buildings in Oxford Circus was released to the press on 22 October 1940. (Historic Military Press)

Above left: At 20.02 hours on the evening of 14 October 1940, a bomb fell in Balham High Road. It penetrated 32ft underground and exploded just above the cross passage between the two platforms of Balham Underground Station. A total of 68 people were killed. This bus, travelling in the blackout, fell into the resulting crater. (Historic Military Press)

Above right: Firemen play their hoses on a still smouldering block of London offices and shops circa 7 October 1940. Note how the censor has blocked out any identifying signs. (Historic Military Press)

Chapter 11

The Beams Crossed Over Coventry

S hortly after 22.00 hours on the evening of 21 June 1940, an Avro Anson of the Blind Approach Training and Development Unit took off from RAF Wyton in Huntingdonshire. Its crew was about to make a discovery that would, in time, prove vital to the British war effort. Denis Richards explained:

[Fitted in the Anson's cabin was] a wireless set of a type used by the American police. It was specially designed to receive frequencies in the neighbourhood of 30 megacycles per second [mcs]. The pilot, who had re-joined the unit the previous day, was a little vague about the object of the exercise. He was clear enough, however, about his immediate orders, which were to attempt to find a beam signal on frequencies 30, 31.5 or 33 mcs.

Though the weather was murky below, the aircraft was soon clear of the clouds, and at 10,000 feet, under the starry canopy of the midsummer night sky, the search began. It was not long before the wireless operator – a peacetime radio enthusiast who continued to twiddle his knobs with the chevrons of a Royal Air Force corporal on his sleeve – picked up very loud and clear signals on 30 mcs. They consisted of dashes repeated sixty times a minute – as in the British standard beam-approach and the German Lorenz system for blind landing.

This was promising, and the pilot headed north with high hopes. About twenty miles beyond Wyton, the dashes changed into a continuous note. The aircraft was in the beam. It proved to be less than half a mile wide, with very clearly defined dot and dash edges; and by keeping towards one edge the pilot found that he could fly along it with an accuracy of 100–200 yards. Having confirmed his position from a 'fix', the navigator then plotted the path of the beam. In one direction it extended towards Western Germany,

A view of Coventry after the passing of the German bombers during the Blitz. This photograph was taken from Little Park Street. At least six people died in Little Park Street in the Blitz, though only one during Operation *Moonlight Sonata* in November 1940. The remainder, all members of the AFS, were killed or fatally injured there in an attack on 11 April 1941. (Historic Military Press)

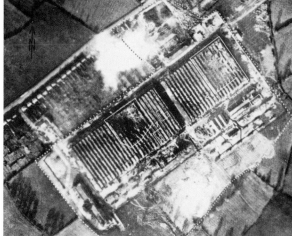

Above left and above right: A pair of Luftwaffe aerial reconnaissance photographs show an unidentified factory in Coventry before, and then after, the attack on 14 November 1940. All the original caption states is that it was 'an aircraft factory'. (National Museum of Denmark)

whence in fact it was originating; and in the other, doubtless for reasons not unconnected with the presence of the Rolls-Royce aero-engine works, it passed across the town of Derby.[1]

Having returned to Wyton, the results of the Anson's flight were immediately passed to Professor R V Jones. As a scientist working in the Intelligence Section of the Air Ministry, Jones played an important role in the defence of Britain during World War Two. He also knew exactly what had been discovered that night – the beams were part of a blind-flying navigation system known to the enemy as *Knickebein* ('crooked leg'). Using this, a German bomber flew along a beam until it was intersected by second beam, at which moment a different note sounded in the operator's earphones. This indicated that the aircraft was over the target, at which point its deadly cargo was sent on its way.

When the German bombers set out on their missions on the evening of Thursday, 14 November 1940, they knew that the beams would, as usual, cross over their target – in this case the engineering and armaments producing city of Coventry.

A Night of Terror

The war had already visited the Midlands' industrial centre, which had been raided 17 times already in September and October. Though the sights and sounds of war had, therefore become familiar to the people of Coventry, nothing that had gone before prepared them for what was about to happen when, shortly before 19.00 hours, the sirens began to wail.

For their attack, the raiders were led by 13 specially modified Heinkel He 111s of Kampfgruppe 100, which were equipped with X-Gerät navigational devices, these being a subsequent and more accurate development of the *Knickebein* system. These aircraft dropped their marker flares at 19.20 hours, pointing the way for Luftflotte 3's force of 515 bombers.

On the ground, John Bailey watched the flares floating down: 'Rows of them seemed to hang suspended in the sky and remined me of the fairy lights of a coronation. Suddenly, a terrific hissing was heard as thousands of incendiary bombs fell… when the flare of these firebombs died, we could see the glare of the burning houses.'[2] Coventry's night of terror had just begun.

'The bombs were dropping virtually before the siren sounded', remembered 11-year-old Paul Strike, 'and it was not long before our house was badly damaged, with us all taking up cramped refuge under the stairs. I shall never be able to forget the sound of the German bombers and the hell that erupted when the bombs started falling.'[3]

1. Denis Richards, *Royal Air Force 1939-1945*, Vol. I (HMSO, London, 1953), p.198.
2. David McGrory, *Coventry's Blitz* (Amberley, Stroud, 2015), p.60.
3. BBC People's War website, Article ID: A2036981.

Reginald Tweed had gone to the Roxy Cinema on Foleshill Road that evening with a friend. When the siren sounded, the filmgoers were told to go to the public air raid shelters outside. These were concrete and brick structures that would be secure against incendiaries and bomb-case splinters, but they would have offered scant protection against a direct hit: 'At 7pm the German bombers came, first there were hundreds of flares, which lit up the full moon, then hundreds of incendiary firebombs. Everywhere was on fire, then came the cascade of bombs and land mines. My first thought was, if I survived the bombs, I would be burnt alive. There were horrific sounds of raging fires all around.'[4]

Moonlight Sonata

The objectives of the German raid, code-named Operation *Mondscheinsonate* (or *Moonlight Sonata*) after the famous Beethoven composition, was to destroy Coventry's factories and industrial infrastructure, though it was inevitable that the rest of Coventry was liable to be severely damaged.

Throughout the course of the raid, the Germans dropped about 500 tonnes of high explosives and 36,000 incendiary bombs. Such a high concentration of missiles in so confined an area meant that most of Coventry's inhabitants heard, or felt, the fall of many of the bombs. There was no question of the attack moving from one part of the city to another some distance away. Every moment of the onslaught bore down on almost every part the centre of the city and its nearer environs, something that the people of the sprawling metropolis were never called on to endure.

One woman was on her way home that evening when the air raid siren sounded:

Within minutes all hell was let loose – bombs whistling and falling, fires starting, buildings rocking and crashing down all around – and a policeman blowing his whistle and shouting urgently 'Take cover, take cover – get off the streets, get off the streets!' I dived through the big glass doors of the Gaumont cinema and just as I did so a big bomb hit the building, causing the ceiling to fall and the glass doors to shatter. I was blown over and partially buried. The blast caught the people sheltering in the stalls and the upper circle collapsed on to them. Many were injured, some were dead. We struggled and pulled people out from under the rubble, and to this day I can remember how a young woman had her arms round her unconscious RAF husband (they had been married that morning) with his blood all over her brand-new wedding coat. We lined the injured up in the partial shelter of an undamaged foyer wall – hoping for an ambulance and rendering what little aid we could. Another enormous crash and the lights went out. This was not as desperate as it sounds because the buildings all around were on fire from cellar to attic, flames meeting across the road and lighting up the whole area as if

---

4. BBC People's War website, Article ID: A4896796.

Above left: **The badly damaged Ford's Hospital in Coventry's Greyfriars Lane after it was hit by bombs in the Blitz. Note the large wooden supports holding up the walls. The damage seen here was actually caused before Operation *Moonlight Sonata*, on 14 October 1940. (Historic Military Press)**

Above right: **The centre of Coventry after the Luftwaffe's Blitz. The distinctive structure in the foreground is the 100ft-high Market Hall Clock Tower. Rendered unsafe in the attack on 14 November, it was demolished in 1942. (Historic Military Press)**

it was broad daylight. An ambulance crept towards us over the rubble, potholes and broken water mains, through the inferno. We stopped it and carried, pushed, pulled and led about 15 people into it, slammed the doors and watched it go.[5]

The Cathedral

The building that was to become both the reminder of the devastation wrought by the bombing of 14 November, and the symbol of the city's regeneration, is the Cathedral of St Michael. Largely constructed between the late 14th century and early 15th century, it was one of the largest parish churches in England when, in 1918, it was elevated to cathedral status on the creation of Coventry Diocese.

As the Luftwaffe appeared in the skies over the city on 14 November, the first incendiaries landed on the cathedral at 19.40 hours. One fell on the roof of the chancel and another broke through the roof and fell onto the nave by the lectern. A call went out for the fire brigade while the cathedral staff led by the provost quickly moved into action. The incendiary that fell on the chancel roof was flipped onto the ground and the one in the nave was smothered with two buckets of sand.

At around this point, another incendiary landed on the roof of the south aisle above the organ and burnt through the lead and fell onto the old timbers which caught fire. Four men managed to bring the fire under control. But then a further stick of incendiaries landed on the cathedral and created fires that the men there, with nothing more than buckets of water and sand to fight the flames with, could not control.

Shortly after this, the high explosive bombs began to fall. Windows were blown out, and more fires were started, which once again the men had no chance of subduing. The fire brigade was urgently needed, but with virtually the whole of the city on fire, every fireman and every appliance were battling fires throughout the city and throughout the night. It was not until 21.30 hours that the Solihull Fire Brigade arrived. Before then, with no chance of saving the building, the men decided to try and rescue as many objects as they could carry out of the cathedral. Crosses, candlesticks and chalices were whisked away, as well as the Colours of the Royal Warwickshire Regiment.

---

5. BBC People's War website, Article ID: A2110906.

Above left: Residents and ARP personnel gather among the rubble and debris from the bombing in Coventry's city centre. In the background is the tower and spire of Holy Trinity parish church. The church survived the attack of 14 November through the efforts of the vicar, Rev Graham Clitheroe, and a dedicated team of fire-watchers. They had been sleeping in the North Porch when the bombing started and went on to spend the rest of the night 'extinguishing fires around the building and even pushing bombs off the church roof to stop further damage'. (via Historic Military Press)

Above right: Wounded US servicemen pictured in the ruins of Coventry Cathedral during a Mothers' Day service held on 13 May 1945. The men were all patients in nearby convalescent hospitals. The service was also attended by the mayor of Coventry. (NARA)

Shortly after the firemen unrolled their hoses and started to attack the fires raging throughout the building, the water supply failed. It did not come back until around 22.30 hours, and, even then, the pressure was low. The bombing had busted open water pipes and demolished hydrants. By this time, the cathedral was rapidly being destroyed. 'The whole interior was a seething mass of flame and piled-up blazing beams and timbers, interpenetrated and surmounted with dense bronze-coloured smoke', explained the provost. 'Through this could be seen the concentrated blaze caused by the burning of the organ, famous for its long history back to the time when Handel played upon it.'[6]

A Deadly Rescue

It was not just the water mains that had been put out of action by the German bombs, the electricity and gas supplies were also cut, as PC Wilfred Lambert recalled: 'When I went to the [police] station, the doors were flying backwards and forwards by the terrific blast that was going through the building, like a whirlwind. Most of the windows had been blown out and the blinds were flapping. Nearly all our telephones had been put out of action, so that the few reports that came through were delivered by hand.' One of those reports was of a shelter under a business premises that had been hit, trapping 14 people inside.

---

6. *Coventry's Blitz* (Coventry Newspapers, 1990), p.6.

Winston Churchill walking through the ruined nave of Coventry Cathedral on 28 September 1941. (Library of Congress)

A rescue team was formed of Inspector Ward, three constables, including PC Lambert, and four specials. They reached Smith's, a furnishers, and began pulling away at the rubble. Most of the digging was done by the police officers.

With their jackets off and shirt sleeves rolled up, they tunnelled under huge piles of masonry with spades and pickaxes. After about an hour of exhausting endeavour, they had still not reached the trapped people, and it was evident that more help was needed. Lambert volunteered to go back to the station to round up more men. He had just reached the station when Inspector Ward staggered towards him – the rescue party had been hit by a bomb and, apart from the inspector, had all been killed: 'I went with him and saw all five of the rescue party lying on top of a heap of bricks and debris. They were all blackened and burnt, but recognisable.'[7]

Wards Without Windows

The staff at the Coventry and Warwickshire Hospital had the most difficult night of their careers. The house governor later submitted a detailed report on that terrible night:

> Two big fires were started, and the emergency dressing store, which adjoins a ward block, was hit by incendiaries and the fire spread rapidly. Almost immediately, the main dressing store was also hit and was soon blazing fiercely. Onwards throughout the night bombing was incessant. We fought fires in various wards, patients were moved from one building to another – always just in time, and miraculously there were no casualties among the hospital patients or staff.
>
> Soon after midnight the electric current failed: operations were continued in three theatres with the emergency lighting. The windows of two theatres were blown in: it was too cold to continue operating in these, but work was carried on in the one remaining theatre.
>
> As the night wore on it became bitterly cold in all the wards, as every window had long since been blown out: extra blankets were issued. Every few moments we had to throw ourselves on the floor as tremendous explosions shook the buildings. The one operating theatre in use could not cope with the large number of cases transferred from the reception hall, and casualties covered almost every foot of floor space in the lower rooms and corridors.
>
> The staff and patients were magnificent. There was never a sign of panic, and several of the male patients were continuously in the grounds, putting out incendiary bombs. In one ward, badly shattered by a high explosive bomb less than 20 yards away, patients who could not be moved were lying in their beds and watching the aeroplanes in the sky, which was aglow from the fires in the city.[8]

---

7. McGrory, op cit, p.72.
8. *The Times*, 23 November 1940.

The shell of Coventry Cathedral after Operation *Moonlight Sonata*. Work to remove the rubble and debris is still ongoing. (Historic Military Press)

Maurice Rattigan and his family were in their back-garden shelter. 'About midnight there was a terrific explosion nearby', he remembered, 'and the blast rushed through the shelter hitting us, blowing out the candles and lifting the slab off the emergency exit. A parachute mine had landed about 180 yards away at the back of houses nearby… Cautiously leaving the shelter, we could hear screams and crying coming from distant houses which had been damaged.' The occupants from one of the houses that had been damaged were advised to go to a public shelter for the rest of the night. Later, that shelter received a direct hit and all eight people inside were killed.[9]

Even the German aircrew quickly realised the effects of their attack. Günther Unger, a German pilot who flew against Coventry that night, describes how, even as the bombers from Luftflotte 3 were crossing the Channel, they saw a small pinpoint of white light ahead, like a hand torch. 'As we drew closer to our target,' he later recalled, 'the light gradually became larger until suddenly it dawned on us: we were looking at the burning city of Coventry'.[10]

The Morning After

There were numerous mentions of the rate of fire of the anti-aircraft guns that put up an almost unceasing barrage, even though the city boasted less than 40 anti-aircraft guns, and these were surrounding the city rather than being placed in the centre, while Coventry also had only 50 barrage balloons. One such account was given by Marcus Sadler, in a letter to his father in Sutton Coldfield: 'The anti-aircraft fire was terrific, with the tracer shells from the smaller guns cutting queer white lines through the sky, and the Bofors guns were shooting up flares, and wire mesh traps to try and catch the diving planes. Machine guns on the ground were shooting at other flares from the planes and also potting at big 2-ton land mines floating down slowly

9.   BBC People's War website, Article ID: A4212758.
10. Ronald Lewin, *Ultra Goes To War* (Pen & Sword, Barnsley, 2008), p.103.

The 'Charred Cross' on display at Coventry Cathedral. Following the bombing, the cathedral's stonemason, Jock Forbes, saw two wooden beams lying in the shape of a cross and tied them together. The original is now displayed by the stairs linking the cathedral with St Michael's Hall below. (Courtesy of Jim Linwood)

by 30ft span parachutes.'[11] It has been estimated that 6,700 rounds were fired by the anti-aircraft guns, however, only one German raider was shot down.

At 06.16 hours, Coventry received the 'Raiders Passed' signal. However, due to the damaged electricity supply, most of the air raid sirens could not pass the 'All Clear' signal to the shell-shocked population. Many people had to be told by passing police and Air Raid Wardens that the devastating raid was actually over.

Stunned with the intensity of the attack during the night, the heaviest on any city outside London, the people of Coventry were then shocked with the sights that greeted them the following day as they emerged from their shelters and places of refuge. Many people wondered around, either totally bewildered by the destruction of their hometown, or simply trying to find their bearings and recognise a street, or just a single building, so they could work out where to go.

Tom Lines, a Home Guard volunteer, wrote of what he saw as he made his way into the centre of the city on the 15th:

> We saw one street where houses on one side still stood and, although many were damaged, they could probably be repaired. We could see houses with roofs missing or shattered – open to the skies and bad weather. Blackout material and curtains flapped, torn and tattered. The awful destruction and mess was terrible to see… to witness all this sad destruction was hard to believe. Telegraph poles were bent at crazy angles, overhead tram lines were broken, and piles of bricks were still smoking.[12]

More than 41,000 houses were damaged that night, with 2,306 destroyed or demolished – almost one-third of the city's houses were left uninhabitable – and 35 per cent of its shops destroyed. Given the concentration of bombs that fell on such a comparatively confined area, casualty figures, though tragic in each instance, were relatively low, with just 568 being killed and around 1,000 injured. In a relatively small city with a population of just over 200,000, it is said that everyone knew someone killed or injured that night.

Of the 180 factories in the city, the main targets of the German bombers, nearly all were reported to have been damaged to one extent or another; 75 were destroyed. Among the latter were two vehicle factories, a machine tool works, nine aircraft factories, and two naval ordnance stores.

A New Verb

Such was the utter devastation wrought during the attack on 14 November, that a new verb entered the English language. Delighted with the destruction the Luftwaffe had caused, the German propaganda ministry coined a new word – 'Coventrieren' or to 'Coventrate' – which, most dictionary definitions agree, means to 'devastate by heavy bombing'.

Yet for all the damage that was done to the city and its factories, the effect on war production was only temporary, as much essential work had already been moved to 'shadow factories' on Coventry's outskirts. Within a few months, the factories in the city were rebuilt and back to full production.

---

11. See www.ourwarwickshire.org.uk.
12. *Coventry's Blitz* (Coventry Newspapers, 1990), p.9.

Chapter 12

The Secret War Against the Blitz

For the *Knickebein* and other beam navigation systems to work, the German bomber crews needed to know some basic information on the beams and their directions. The Luftwaffe sent information this data via encrypted radio messages. These radio signals were picked up by the British Signals Intelligence Y-Stations and passed onto the men and women of the Government Code and Cypher School at Bletchley Park. Under the colour coding of 'Brown' for these Enigma decrypts, a team quickly got to work on cracking the messages as part of what has come to be known as the 'Battle of the Beams'.

The operatives of Hut 6 at Bletchley Park succeeded in achieving this. Soon, the Air Ministry was receiving vital information concerning potential German raids and the number of bombers that might be involved. Thanks to Enigma, as one veteran of the Government Code and Cypher School, Oliver Lawn, noted, the Air Ministry also had the wherewithal to 'bend' the German navigation beams, thereby causing the Luftwaffe's aircraft to drop their loads in the wrong places:

> One of the things the Germans used the Enigma machine for, in the early stages of the war, was directing their bombing of British cities – beam bombing. That's an aeroplane going along a beam and another beam being sent to cross it. And that was the point at which they dropped their bombs, over the centre of the city. Now, there was a code which set the angles of the beams. And if you could break the code, clever engineers could bend one of the beams so that the crossing point was over green fields, and not over cities.[1]

The information Bletchley supplied was never conclusive, but it was possible to identify units and call signs and thus report on numbers. However, in 1940, Bletchley Park was not able to accurately identify disguised place names in messages. For that, what was needed was a codebook, as aliases could only be guessed at.

Thus, the efforts at Bletchley took on a new urgency. The movement of troops and similar information gleaned from the Enigma signals was one thing, the bombing of ordinary citizens in large cities was another altogether. It was against this backdrop that myth has developed involving Bletchley Park.

Through a 'Brown' message decrypt from Enigma on 11 November 1940, the codebreakers were able to tell Air Intelligence that a heavy German raid was imminent. The codename given to this raid was, as we have already seen, Operation *Mondscheinsonate* (*Moonlight Sonata*). The German aircraft would be led by navigation beams, and there was a list of four potential targets, each of which also had been given codenames. One of the codenames was *Korn*.

Shortly before this information was obtained, a German prisoner of war whose conversation had been monitored, had stated that a heavy raid was planned for Birmingham or Coventry. Then, on 12 November 1940, a 'Brown' Enigma decrypt appeared to give details on navigation beams showing that three of the potential targets were the heavily industrialised cities of Birmingham, Wolverhampton and Coventry. The date for the raid was most likely to be around 15 November.

With this information supplied by Bletchley Park, Air Intelligence reported to the Prime Minister on the morning of Thursday, 14 November 1940, informing him that the target was possibly London (given the

---

1. Quoted by Sinclair McKay, *The Secret Life of Bletchley Park: The WWII Codebreaking Centre and the Men and Women who Worked There* (Aurum Press, London, 2010), p.97.

Bletchley Park's Hut 6, seen here in 2004, housed the team tasked with breaking the German Army and Air Force Enigma-enciphered wireless traffic. The adjacent Hut 3, meanwhile, handled the translation and intelligence analysis of the raw decrypts provided by Hut 6.

sheer size of the raid planned), but that it could also be either Coventry or Birmingham – after all, no one at that stage knew what the codeword *Korn* signified.

By 15.00 hours that day, further intercepted radio signals made it evident that Coventry was to be the target, and that the raid was to take place that very night. Why then, some people question, were the people of Coventry given no warning of what was about to happen to them? Why was no attempt made to stop a raid that resulted in the dropping of thousands of incendiaries and tons of high explosives, creating a raging fire that destroyed almost everything within the radius of a quarter-of-a-mile, including the city's cathedral?

The reason, it is frequently said, is that to have deflected the bombing by sabotaging the navigation beams, or by allowing Fighter Command to defend the city from the air, would have been a clear indication to the Germans that Britain had access to their most secret communications. Churchill was, therefore, faced with the most difficult of decisions. Should he intervene and order all measures to be taken to protect Coventry and in doing so jeopardise his most important secret weapon, or instead should he allow the city to be attacked? It is claimed by some that Churchill left Coventry to its fate to protect the great secret of Bletchley Park.

The facts, however, reveal a somewhat different picture. On the day in question, Churchill set off for a country house in Ditchley, Oxfordshire, where he often stayed, rather than Chequers, on moonlit nights. When he was told that there was to be a large raid that night and that the target might be London, he returned to the capital – Churchill was determined not to be absent from his post when the capital was bombed. It was only when he arrived back at Whitehall in the evening that it was finally confirmed that the target was likely to be Coventry.

Another who would have known in advance that Coventry was the Luftwaffe's target for that Thursday evening in November 1940 was the government scientist Professor R V Jones. But, writing after the war, he asserted that, 'I myself did not know in advance specifically that Coventry was the target when I went home in the evening of 14th November'. Indeed, he recalls driving through west London that afternoon 'wondering where the target really was'.[2]

Peter Calvocoressi was head of the Air Section at Bletchley Park, which translated and analysed all deciphered Luftwaffe messages. He later confirmed that, '*Ultra* never mentioned Coventry... Churchill, so far from pondering whether to save Coventry or safeguard *Ultra*, was under the impression that the raid was to be on London'.[3]

It has also been stated that when it was eventually realised that Coventry was indeed the target, with barely hours to go, its residents were not informed about the raid and therefore given no opportunity to evacuate the city. This is discussed by one of the women at Bletchley Park, Aileen Clayton. 'Coventry could never have been evacuated in time', she declared. 'It would certainly have been a physical impossibility to get all the guns and searchlights needed for defence, as well as the fire engines and other equipment, moved from other places... with the information that was available to us, there was no way in which the city and its people could have been saved from that suffering.'

Another who was at Bletchley at that time was Captain Frederick Winterbotham: 'It seemed to me, sitting in my office a little weary after the sleepless bomb-torn night before, that there would be absolute chaos if everyone tried to get out of the city in the few hours available and that if, for any reason, the raid was postponed by weather or for some other reason, we should have put the source of our information at risk to no purpose.'

It would seem that the claim that Churchill abandoned Coventry to its fate that night was due in part to Winterbotham and his book, *The Ultra Secret*, which was published in 1974. Of this action, Winterbotham stated: 'This is the sort of terrible decision that sometimes has to be made on the highest levels in war. It was unquestionably the right one.'

There was little, then, that could be done to save Coventry. The tragedy of the events that night really resulted from the fact that the raid took place in 1940. This was a year in which the breaking of the German codes was far from complete (a situation compounded by contradictory and uncertain intelligence), German tactics were evolving and changing, and the British defences (both on the ground and in the air) had yet to reach full strength and operational efficiency. Quite simply, on that day in 1940 events had conspired against the city.

The Battle of the Beams

Knowing about the beams was one thing – the ultimate aim for the defenders was, as Oliver Lawn had pointed out, to interrupt them, or, better still, bend them, thereby deflecting the bombers from their target. This gave rise to what has become known as the Battle of the Beams.

The first victory achieved by the British followed the Avro Anson flight on 21 June 1940. By September 1940, when the Blitz was unleashed, countermeasures against *Knickebein* had been put in place. Put simply, R V Jones and his team were operating powerful transmitters that 'degraded *Knickebein* signals by injecting them with Morse code patterns', thereby confusing the German crews. Since the beams were codenamed *Headaches*, the transmitters came to be known as *Aspirins*.

Though *Knickebein* had been neutralised, by the time of the Coventry attack in November 1940, the Germans had begun using a new beam system known as X-Gerät. It proved a harder nut to crack than its predecessor.

The breakthrough came on 6 November 1940, when a Heinkel He 111 fitted with the system crashed near Bridport, enabling the scientists to discover its secrets. Though X-Gerät was initially disrupted by using modified jammers from the *Knickebein* effort, a more permanent solution was the introduction of equipment that produced a fake beam that would cross the main navigation beam, thereby tricking the bombers into releasing their deadly cargo sooner than had been intended.

As the British slowly gained the upper hand in the Battle of the Beams, the Germans began a third phase in the deployment of their beam navigation systems, one which centred on the Y-Gerät equipment.

---

2. Ronald Lewin, *Ultra Goes To War* (Pen & Sword, Barnsley, 2008), p.101.
3. Peter Calvocoressi, *Top Secret Ultra* (Ballantine Books, New York, 1981), pp.85–86.

Despite the successes of the Battle of the Beams, the bombers still got through. St John Horsleydown was the parish church of Horsleydown in Bermondsey. It was severely damaged by a single bomb on 20 September 1940. The church was completely closed in 1964 and the building demolished down to floor level, which was then used as the footings for the London City Mission. (Courtesy of Robert Mitchell)

This, though, was no great surprise to Jones and his staff, as both Enigma decrypts provided by Bletchley Park and earlier intelligence had already alluded to its existence.

Y-Gerät provided a complicated signal that a Luftwaffe bomber with the proper equipment could use to stay on its path to the target. 'However', notes the author Greg Goebel, 'the navigation system also transmitted a second signal, which the bomber's equipment re-radiated on a slightly different frequency. The phase difference between the original and re-radiated signal increased as the bomber flew away from the transmitter, giving an indication of range. When the bomber was over the target, the flight crew were told by radio to drop their bombs.'[4]

To combat this latest threat, the British needed a transmitter powerful enough and with the right frequencies. As it turned out, the Germans had made a fundamental mistake when selecting the frequency for Y-Gerät – it turned out to be the same as the BBC's national television broadcasting station at Alexandra Palace in London. With the television service having been halted on the outbreak of war, the site was dormant and therefore ideally suited for Jones' work.

Alexandra Palace was immediately put to work picking up the Y-Gerät transmissions and, as Greg Goebel concludes, 'in conjunction with supporting ground stations, shoot them back on the same frequency at high power. This jamming system was in place by the end of February 1941 and confused the Luftwaffe considerably. [Y-Gerät] was jammed the very first time it was used in combat, and British listening stations overheard angry remarks from Luftwaffe crews back to their ground controllers. More sophisticated jammers would be developed in a few months.'

The British had won the Battle of the Beams. It was now down to the other defensive measures, such as the anti-aircraft guns and night fighters, to further cement a victory over the bombers.

---

4. See: http://vc.airvectors.net/ttwiz_07.html.

Chapter 13

Battling the Blitz

As the Luftwaffe had, until the afternoon of 7 September 1940, been concentrating on destroying the RAF's airfields, London found itself thinly defended by the Anti-Aircraft Command. In fact, the entire capital was protected by a paltry 92 heavy guns when the bombers appeared over the East End that afternoon.

As soon as Göring's intentions became apparent, General Sir Frederick Pile, General Officer Commanding-in-Chief, Anti-Aircraft Command, reacted swiftly. Within 48 hours, there were 203 heavy guns in and around London, as well as numerous light guns. The effect was quickly felt, as noted Pile when compiling his official despatch in December 1947:

> By day, though it was impossible for the RAF to prevent the Germans reaching the capital, and though when they were there it was too late to prevent them bombing the city, the guns destroyed a considerable number in many of the formations. It was significant too that the most spectacular success which the enemy achieved by day, namely the firing of the dock area on 7th September 1940, occurred when the gun defences were numerically at their lowest ebb.

Engaging the bombers in daylight when they were often visible was one thing, achieving the same results at night, following the Luftwaffe's switch to nocturnal operations, was an altogether different proposition, even when searchlights were available. The sound detectors then in use were proving too inaccurate, and the tracking of the raiders too complicated and unreliable.

As early as 11 September 1940, Pile, in desperation, instructed many of his guns that they had 'a free hand to use any method of [gun] control they liked'.

> The volume of fire which resulted, and which was publicized as a 'barrage', was in fact largely wild and uncontrolled shooting. There were, however, two valuable results from it: the volume of fire had a deterrent effect upon at least some of the German aircrews, so that, though it cannot be proved by records, I have

A heavy anti-aircraft battery stands ready to engage German bombers during the Blitz. (Historic Military Press)

Above left: **Members of the public watch as an anti-aircraft gun crew goes through its paces in Hyde Park, London, on the eve of war in the summer of 1939. (NARA)**

Above right: **A sound detector in action during 1939 or 1940. Equipment such as this proved to be of little value in combating the Luftwaffe's night raids in the Blitz. (National Museum of Denmark)**

every reason to believe that one-third failed to reach their objective; there was also a marked improvement in civilian morale.

The breakthrough for the anti-aircraft gunners came on 1 October 1940 when, for the first time, radar was first used to control anti-aircraft gunfire. The first sets had actually been received at the end of 1939, but a delay in applying them to anti-aircraft work had been caused by their complete inability to give any indication of the height of the aircraft. Thankfully, a solution had been found by the autumn of 1940.

As the weeks of the Blitz passed, the amount of radar equipment available rapidly increased, with improved and more advanced sets also being issued – not just in London, but nationwide. Even searchlight batteries started, at Pile's insistence, to be equipped with radar. It was a period in which, recalled Pile, 'developments in technique were very considerable'.

The results of these improvements quickly became apparent. Concluding his account of the part his guns played in the Blitz, Pile stated:

As in every other aspect of the war, so in the air war the Germans changed their tactics as soon as it became evident that we had gained the upper hand. So, while the preparations they had to make for the Russian campaign no doubt influenced the decision, there is no doubt the German General Staff had by May, 1941, come to the conclusion that the war was not to be won by aerial attacks on this country and that the cost of such attacks was heavy. Between 1st April and 12th May, 1941, the successes scored by the guns mounted steadily. During this month and a half, 72 planes were destroyed by night by the guns and 82 probably destroyed or damaged.

Raining Steel
As the Blitz progressed, most residents of Britain's towns and cities quickly discovered one distinctly unpleasant side-effect of the anti-aircraft guns when they opened up. Quite simply, what goes up must come

down. One such person was Colin Perry, who, as a teenager, kept a detailed diary throughout the bombing of London in 1940. One of his first recollections of his experiences at the hands of the defending anti-aircraft guns was noted on 12 September 1940:

The sirens blasted at 8.34 last night, and straight away an intense anti-aircraft barrage was thrown up. It was impossible to cross from the shelter to the flat (only at the most 18 yards) for fear of shrapnel. In one lull I did finally achieve the crossing, but was marooned in the hall for twenty minutes whilst our guns fired. After midnight I tried to get to sleep. The guns crashed incessantly… As I tried to sleep the pitter-patter of falling shrapnel (great jagged pieces of iron flung through the air with the energy to kill a man) disturbed my dreams, and when some came in the shelter doorway I wanted to rush and secure a red-hot souvenir, but to have stood in the doorway would have been suicidal.[1]

On 1 October, Colin experienced a far more serious situation when an anti-aircraft shell, having failed to detonate at height, fell complete in the street near his flat. There, it finally decided to explode. Yet the danger crept even closer, as Colin noted in his diary entry for 16 October 1940:

Near midnight there was a terrific din, and all our guns, it seemed to me, were clatter crash bang and bang bang bang. A shower of shrapnel flew around, clattering like hell on the rubbish heap. A shell slid through the air with a scream. Suddenly a crash, a tinkle of glass, I looked all round but saw no sign. This morning, though, I found in the front bedroom the bottom of a shell which had smashed clean through the front bedroom window, and but for the loosely hanging blackout curtains would have hit Dad in bed.[2]

Another London resident who recalled the effects of the shell fragments was Geoff Bawcutt. A schoolboy at the time, he lived through most of the war with his parents in Grove Park, Lewisham. When interviewed in 2004, he remarked:

I can clearly remember the devastating effect that the shrapnel from our anti-aircraft shells caused to the residents in our road… Every time the German aircraft actually appeared during a raid, our anti-aircraft guns would open up. As soon as this happened the air would become full of red-hot pieces of shrapnel, followed by the ping-ping sound of these shards hitting the ground. At times it sounded as if was 'raining' shrapnel. Not one house in the street would escape damage – and the bigger the house, the more the damage. Following each barrage every house would have suffered broken tiles, and if more than one or two tiles next to each other had been smashed, then the roof invariably started to leak. We also had a lean-to garage on the side of the house, and this had a roof of corrugated asbestos material, which, as the blitz progressed, became increasingly peppered with holes caused by the shrapnel. The anti-aircraft guns themselves, and not only the shells they fired, also caused damage to our houses. One day a battery of mobile anti-aircraft guns took up position on the waste ground opposite our houses. Unfortunately, when they opened fire during the next attack the sheer blast from their firing blew in some of the windows at the front of the houses!

Geoff also recalls the youthful exuberance for collecting shrapnel:

We used to go round after the air raids with buckets, gathering the shrapnel so that it could be melted down and recycled. I remember that I once found one lump lying in the street that was as large as my two hands when side-by-side. On another occasion we had been outside watching a raid when I ran over and picked up a piece of shrapnel that fell nearby. I forgot that it would still be red hot and so I got burnt hands for my efforts!

---

1. Quoted from Colin Perry, *Boy in the Blitz: the 1940 Diary of Colin Perry* (Leo Cooper, London, 1972).
2. ibid.

Barbara Nixon, who had the distinction of being Britain's first full-time female Air Raid Warden, would later write of her experiences of wartime London. She spent the worst parts of 1940 and 1941 serving at Post 13 in the London Borough of Finchley. In her memoir, she describes how the anti-aircraft barrage provided its own risks. The following, by way of an example, took place one night in May 1941:

> I got back to our Post to find an oil bomb had fallen on a building thirty yards away, and four floors were blazing. Fire-watchers had already informed the Fire Brigade… This new fire was uncomfortably close to the Post, and was spreading rapidly, although, in this case, there was, intermittently, a small supply of water. A firework display of shrapnel twinkled overhead. But shrapnel was one of the things about which we had all very quickly developed the old soldier's knowledgeableness, and I duly crossed the road and stood in a doorway, till the bits came down with their sighing whistle, and tinkled on the pavements.[3]

The scenes witnessed by Colin Perry, Geoff Bawcutt and Barbara Nixon were by no means confirmed to London. One housewife living in Tennyson Road, Stoke, found that as the night raids wore on, she developed the ability to distinguish between the terrifying sounds emanating from outside: 'High Explosive bombs were easy to distinguish… the clatter of incendiaries on the concrete were… now familiar'. She later recalled that a strange 'hissing noise' was much more puzzling, until she realized that it was the sound of 'the nose caps from the hot anti-aircraft shells as they fell in the rainwater tanks'.

Aged just 16, Fire-watcher George Ashman was working for a company based in Brentwood during the night attacks of the Blitz. He once recalled:

> It had been quite a heavy raid on London, and when we took over at midnight there were bombs falling all round us. So we spent most of our time in the shelter just popping our heads up occasionally every few minutes to make sure that the road was okay! At about 3.30 the same morning things quietened down but there was still gunfire coming from the London area. My cousin said to me, 'Let's walk up the road and show them the fire-watchers are still about'. Looking back God knows who the hell was going to see us! We had walked about 50 yards when, all of a sudden, there was a loud whizzing noise through the air just as if something was coming straight for us. Of course, we both dived over the hedge of the nearest front garden – which happened to be a holly hedge, and I can tell you it hurt! As it turned out the whizzing noise happened to be an anti-aircraft shell which had failed on its way up and had travelled back down to earth![4]

Whilst most of these Blitz participants have recalled their encounters with the results of the anti-aircraft guns firing, it was soon discovered that the danger to life and limb was very real. On the night of 17/18 January 1941, the Luftwaffe, for the first time since 1940, planned a large-scale attack on London. This would also be the night that the Ministry of Home Security chose to launch an investigation into the actual causes of the death and injury to London's citizens. Whilst the enemy was ultimately blamed by government officials for almost the entire dead and wounded suffered in the raid, this was not the whole story. The Ministry's report, not making pleasant reading, was stamped 'secret' and 'restricted' and promptly locked away. Contained within its pages was, for possibly the first time, a true indication of exactly how damaging the defending anti-aircraft barrage actually was.

The investigators elected to compare the incidence of casualties caused by three causes: German bombs, shrapnel and anti-aircraft shells. The information was supplied by both the Medical Officers of Health and senior police officers from the 29 Metropolitan boroughs.[5] The responses showed that of the 29 boroughs, only 18 actually suffered casualties during the raid. However, from these figures, the Ministry of Home Security also came to several, more startling, conclusions.

3. Barbara Nixon, *Raiders Overhead* (Gulliver Publishing, Banbury, 1980).
4. Correspondence with G Ashman, March and April 2005.
5. The National Archive, HO 196/15.

Of the 18 boroughs that suffered casualties, 83 per cent reported that some of their dead and seriously wounded were directly caused by anti-aircraft shells. More specifically, the report reveals that a shocking 1 in 5, or 20 per cent, of all the dead and seriously wounded could be directly attributed to the anti-aircraft shells fired by our own guns. If you just consider just the deaths caused that night, 27 per cent of those killed, or 20 persons, were killed by the defending anti-aircraft shells.

When considering the cases of those who were slightly wounded, the figures make equally dire reading. The bombs dropped that night by the Luftwaffe caused 58 slightly wounded casualties, whilst our own anti-aircraft shells slightly injured 31 people – or 35 per cent of the total. That said, it was shells exploding on returning to the ground, as opposed to falling shrapnel, that was almost always the culprit in these instances.

The statistics, however, keep on coming. Of those boroughs that suffered casualties amongst their residents, a staggering 56 per cent, or 10 in total, reported that *all* of their casualties in the raid that night were the result of our own barrage – and nothing whatsoever to do with the Luftwaffe.

Left: The Mayor of London pictured a visit to an anti-aircraft gun position established in front of St Paul's Cathedral. (National Museum of Denmark)

Below left: The wreckage of a Heinkel He 111H-3, that with the werksnummer 5680, on fire at Burmarsh, Kent, on 11 September 1940. The aircraft had been shot down by anti-aircraft fire over London and force-landed at 16.00 hours. The crew of Unteroffizier Hofmann, Feldwebel Heinz Friedrich, Feldwebel George, Unteroffizier Dreyer and Unteroffizier Stirnemann were all captured, though one of the crew (not the pilot) can be seen here being carried away on a stretcher. The aircraft, 1H+CB, was a write-off. Note the triumphantly circling Spitfire and anti-invasion poles. (Historic Military Press)

Below right: A Luftwaffe airman or member of groundcrew points out damage caused by anti-aircraft fire or an RAF fighter during a mission over Britain in 1940/41. (National Museum of Denmark)

Above left: 'Broken glass strewn outside a shoe shop in Leicester Square', following an air raid on the night of 15/16 October 1940. (Historic Military Press)

Above right: Pilot Officer Richard Stevens DFC & Bar. An RAF night fighter pilot in the early Blitz, he was serving in 151 Squadron at the time this portrait was completed. He was awarded the DFC in January 1941, for 'outstanding work in night fighting operations and showed the utmost keenness and determination for operations in all conditions of weather'. His Bar was gained in May 1941. (Historic Military Press)

Roughly a quarter of those killed the night of 17/18 January 1941 were from the ranks of the various Civil Defence organisations. One of the many counted as part of the survey was Constable Robert William Burns.

Caught out in the open in the raid, PC Burns sought shelter in the doorway of 156 London Lane, Bromley. As he waited for a period of calm to continue with his duties, a complete anti-aircraft shell fell in the roadway nearby and exploded. His wounds were so severe that he never recovered, and he died on 16 June 1944.[6]

Night Fighters Enter the Fray

If radar had made a difference for the anti-aircraft gunners, the same would also be true for the RAF's fighter pilots. While many of the RAF's systems of command and control had been well proven in the Battle of Britain, combating the Luftwaffe's night raids provided Fighter Command with many challenges.

To start with, Denis Richards, the RAF's official historian, noted:

The ordinary Hurricane and Spitfire squadrons, or rather their more experienced members, where thus expected to do duty by night as well as day. They were neither properly trained nor equipped for this, nor had the good night-flying facilities at their airfields. In bright moon, the pilots had no great difficulty in taking off, navigating and landing, but dark or cloudy nights brought fearful hazards. Indeed, it often proved impossible to send our fighters into the air in conditions which presented no obstacle at all to the beam assisted German bombers. In sum, our defence against night attack in September 1940, was entirely inadequate.[7]

Between the start of the Blitz and 13 November 1940, the Luftwaffe carried out some 12,000 sorties over Britain. The British night defences, in the same period, were only able to claim a total of 81 enemy aircraft – 54 by the guns, four by the balloon barrage and eight by the fighters. Almost in desperation, a number of schemes, such as the Turbinlite aircraft (in effect a flying searchlight) and the PAC apparatus (a small rocket trailing a steel cable fired up in front of an enemy bomber), were all pitched into the fray.

It was radar, though, that would prove pivotal. On the night of 13/14 August 1940, the first tests were made with a new Air Interception, or AI, radar set – the Mk.IV – which had a maximum range of nearly 4 miles. At the same time as this piece of equipment was proving its worth, the first Bristol Beaufighters

6. Lewis Blake, *Red Alert* (Privately published, London, 1992).
7. Denis Richards, *Royal Air Force 1939-1945* (HMSO, London, 1953), p.203.

began to enter service. Though both were still in their infancy, and numbers available woefully low, at last the RAF had an 'effective AI in an effective aircraft'.

There was one final development that would revolutionise the RAF's battle to beat the bombers. By the summer of 1940, the scientists at the Air Ministry Research Establishment had developed a radar apparatus for long-distance inland tracking. With this equipment, a controller was able to witness a simultaneous presentation of an enemy raider alongside an intercepting night fighter in relation to the surrounding terrain. Officially known as the Ground-Controlled Interception set, or GCI, the first station opened at Shoreham in October 1940.

At a frantic pace, all of these developments were brought together. At the same time, selection for the aircrew was improved, night fighter training adapted (including the creation of a new night fighter Operational Training Unit), and new navigation aids introduced. As a result, as 1940 passed into 1941, the balance of the battle in the night skies over Britain tipped inexorably in the defenders' favour.

Above left: The wreckage of the Junkers Ju 88 that crashed at Stocks Lane, East Wittering, on 20 November 1940. The victor was the night fighter pilot, John 'Cat's Eyes' Cunningham. (Historic Military Press)

Above right: Part of the engine of a Junkers Ju 88 brought down by a night fighter, lying in the garden of a cottage at Partridge Green, West Sussex, after the Blitz on 28 July 1941. Although several cottages were damaged by wreckage, all the occupants escaped injury. The aircraft in question was a Ju 88A, that coded 4D+MK, of 2/KG 30. (Historic Military Press)

Above left: A contemporary wartime depiction of an RAF Bristol Beaufighter night fighter in action during the Blitz. (Historic Military Press)

Above right: John 'Cat's Eyes' Cunningham, a night fighter pilot with 604 Squadron, meets the King at RAF Middle Wallop on Wednesday, 7 May 1941. That evening, Cunningham went on to shoot down a Heinkel He 111, his 12th victory. (Historic Military Press)

Chapter 14

The 'Second Great Fire of London'

O ver the course of the previous two months, Londoners had learned how to live through the nightly terrors of the Blitz. During the day, they carried on their lives almost normally but made sure they were safely ensconced in shelters or cellars before nightfall. An American visiting London on a fact-finding mission remarked on this sudden change that happened each evening: 'The two worlds, the world of peace and the world of war, exist side by side, separated by only a few minutes of twilight.'

That contrast was even more marked on 29 December, for it was a Sunday; many businesses were closed, and, in that bleak midwinter, the cold streets were empty. The calm of that last weekend of 1940, a year that had seen Britain on its knees in June and then stumble to its feet as summer passed to autumn, was the prelude to a new storm that was about to be unleashed upon its capital city. For Britain stood shaky on its legs, reeling from the blows of the enemy and still unsure of where and when the next strike would be delivered.

As evening crept over the quiet city, its population waited for the nightly chorus of the sirens, and bunkered down as best it could, each person knowing that they might never see the dawn. As expected, the call to the shelters came an hour or so after dusk, at 18.08 hours.

The pathfinding Heinkels of Kampfgruppe 100 led the assault, followed by a further 126 machines – Ju 88s from I/KG 51, Do 17s of KGr 606 and more Heinkels from I/KG 28. The bombers were loaded mainly, but not entirely, with incendiaries that night, each aircraft carrying approximately 1,000 of these small but much feared bombs. They were usually packed into containers, which were dropped and opened at a given height. They were not intended to be precision ordnance, the objective being to create fires that were spread over a wide area, stretching the firefighting services beyond their capacity.

St Paul's Cathedral stands defiant among the surrounding fires and destruction during the Luftwaffe attack on 29 December 1940. Taken from the roof of the *Daily Mail*'s building, this image has been described as 'the most famous picture of all time'. (Historic Military Press)

There were two main types of incendiaries: the 1kg and the 2kg bomb. They were made of magnesium alloy with an incendiary compound (thermite) filling. On hitting the ground, a needle was driven into a percussion cap, which ignited the thermite. The heat from this also ignited the magnesium casing, causing an intense heat that would ignite any flammable material that the bomb was in contact with. Some were fitted with a small explosive charge that went off after seven minutes and was intended to deter efforts at dealing with the devices.[1] The maths that night was simple: London was about to be struck with more than 100,000 bombs.

'Bombs Gone'

Kampfgruppe 100's pathfinder force was led by Hauptmann Fredrich Aschenbrenner. It was his Heinkel that spearheaded the latest onslaught on London, as the author David Johnson noted:

[The bombers] kept to their straight, unwavering flight path, droning over south London at a steady three miles per minute. In the leading bomber… Aschenbrenner held the controls with a light but sure touch; from the compartment behind the pilot, the radio operator kept both ears tuned to his headset. Over two minutes had gone since the X-beam's 'advance signal' had been passed, but as the Heinkel's twin engines growled monotonously over Kennington the watchful bomb-aimer and the two gunners could see no signs of life. They could see nothing at all, in fact, except solid cloud. Then the radioman put both hands in his earphones and stiffened. The tone of the radio beam had once again changed suddenly as the aircraft passed over the 'main signal' – Aschenbrenner and his crew were directly over the target. The radio operator tersely announced their arrival via the intercom; a second later the incendiaries fell out of the bomb bay toward the layers of cloud 1,500 feet below. The bomb aimer, his voice edged with tenseness, announced 'Bombs Gone!' into his microphone.[2]

On the same night that President Franklin D Roosevelt delivered his famous speech declaring that the United States of America 'must be the arsenal of democracy', the British capital was about to endure its worst air raid of World War Two.

Right: **Royal Engineers pulling down unsafe buildings in one of London's streets on 30 or 31 December. (Historic Military Press)**

Below: **This is how the roof of London's Guildhall appeared from an apartment across the street the day after the attack on 29 December. The Guildhall was one of many London buildings damaged by fire when air raiders showered the city with incendiary bombs. (Historic Military Press)**

---

1. John Ray, *Night Blitz* (self-published Kindle edition, 2012).
2. David Johnson, *The London Blitz* (Scarborough House, Chelsea, 1990), pp.77–8.

Impossible To Breathe

The incendiaries that fluttered down that Sunday evening from around 18.15 hours were directed not at the docks or factories of the East End, but at the City, aiming to cut communications across the Thames, by destroying train stations, bridges over the river and the main telephone centre on Faraday Street. The jumble of multi-story buildings in this area of the City, bounded by Ludgate Hill, Warwick Lane, Newgate Street and Paternoster Square, were showered with incendiaries, with more than 300 a minute cascading upon the confines of its old, narrow streets.

These small ordnances did not slam into the ground as one might imagine a conventional bomb would. They 'bounced crazily like a football', described one Londoner, 'splutter violently for the first minute, throwing white fire about thirty feet, then simmer down in an intense molten mass and burn about ten minutes more'.

The government's pre-war pamphlet titled *Fire Precautions in War Time*, warned: 'Once a fire gets out of control, you cannot tell how fast it may spread.' It therefore advised that the best way to tackle a fire was in its early stages, stating that as soon as an incendiary landed, every effort by those in the immediate vicinity must be made to smother the flames as quickly as possible. But the next sentence of the government's leaflet proved unfortunately prophetic for Sunday, 29 December: 'However strong the Fire Brigade may be, an outbreak of many fires all close together and beginning at the same time would be more than it could successfully deal with unless the householder himself and his family took the first steps in defending their home.'[3]

Much of the City, London's financial and commercial centre, was composed of business premises and not individual households. Though there was a requirement that many larger places were manned by

---

The Design for the Reconstruction of
All Hallows - by - the - Tower
which was largely destroyed by enemy action in December 1940

"The Glory of this latter House
shall be greater than of the former,
saith the Lord."

Donations to the Restoration Fund should be sent to:
THE HON. TREASURER,
All Hallows Porchroom,
Byward Street,
LONDON, E.C.3.

or to: THE BISHOP OF LONDON'S CHURCH APPEAL,
33 Bedford Square,
LONDON, W.C.1.

and earmarked for All Hallows, Barking-by-the-Tower, (Parish No. 1)

The rear of a fund-raising postcard sold in support of the rebuilding of All Hallows-By-The-Tower church, which was largely destroyed during the Blitz in December 1940. The church is located on Byward Street in the City of London, overlooking the Tower of London. The church was rebuilt after the war, being rededicated in 1957. The vicar at the time was the Reverend 'Tubby' Clayton, founder of the Toc H movement in World War One. (Historic Military Press)

---

3. Quoted in M J Gaskin, *Blitz, The Story of 29th December 1940* (Faber and Faber, London, 2005), pp.197–8.

fire-watching and firefighting teams at night (under the terms of the Fire Watchers Order of September 1940), these teams were small compared to the size of buildings they had to protect, and there was little they could do to quench multiple fires as bundles of incendiaries fell around them. Other smaller buildings were unmanned with no one to unlock their heavy doors to allow firefighters access. By the time the flames had burned through from inside to out, as incendiaries punctured the roofs, often nothing could save these premises from utter ruin.

High explosive bombs followed the incendiaries. Though fewer in number by comparison with the usual loads of the German bombers, they did their job well, bringing structures down to block the efforts of the firefighters trying to reach the burning buildings.

One of those bombs knocked out a vital trunk-mains that carried water to the hydrants in the City. There was no longer anything that the firemen in the centre could do to prevent the flames clawing their way from one building to the next: 'The atmosphere was stifling. A shrivelling blast carried sparks and glowing embers to every corner of the street, sweeping them high into the air.

Left: **The morning after the fire raid of 29 December 1940. Businessmen unable to reach their offices in Fore Street survey the devastation caused the previous night. (Historic Military Press)**

Below left: **A view of Fore Street after the clearance work had begun. The church in the background is St Giles-without-Cripplegate. (Historic Military Press)**

Below right: **The aftermath of an earlier air raid on London in December 1940 – in this case, the 1st of the month. The sign on the wall indicates that this is a Port of London Authority warehouse. (Historic Military Press)**

Firemen, deprived of the protection of their jets, found breathing difficult and were forced back to positions where the air temperature permitted them to fill their lungs freely without searing the air passages.'[4] Added to this problem was that the raid occurred at low tide in the Thames, and soon the fire hoses were getting clogged up with mud.

The Flaming Asphalt

Not all of the thousands of incendiaries that fell that night landed where there was flammable material, many indeed fell on stony ground. But across London as a whole, more than 1,500 fires were started, most being in or around the famous Square Mile.

The appropriately named Commander Sir Aylmer Newton George Firebrace, the London regional Fire Chief, was in the control room at the Red Cross Street fire station, a place long-since lost under the development of the Barbican:

In the control room, a conference is being held by senior London Fire Brigade (LFB) officers. How black – or, more realistically, how red – is the situation, only those who have recently been in the open realise. One by one the telephone lines fail; the heat from the fires penetrates to the control room and the atmosphere is stifling. earlier in the evening, after a bomb falls near, the station lights fail – a few shaded electric hand lamps now supply bright pin-point lights in sharp contrast to a few oil lamps and some perspiring candles.

Taken looking out over London towards Tower Bridge on 10 January 1941, this photograph shows some of the damage that the Luftwaffe attacks had caused. Note the battered railway station top left. (Historic Military Press)

4. Cyril Demarene OBE, *The London Blitz* (After the Battle, London, 1991), p.56.

Viewed from St Paul's Cathedral, this is the area around Paternoster Row, which suffered badly during the attack on 29 December. The domed building is the Old Bailey; the four-turreted tower is that of the Church of St Bartholomew; and the high-spired church on the right is Christ Church. (Historic Military Press)

As the fires crept ever closer, it was evident that the fire station would have to be abandoned. So intense was the heat that the asphalt in the yard of Redcross Street's sub-station burst into flames. Commander Firebrace continued:

> The high wind which accompanies conflagrations is now stronger than ever, and the air is filled with a fierce driving rain of red-hot sparks and burning brands… The clouds overhead are a rose-pink from the reflected glow of the fires, and fortunately it is bright enough to pick our way eastward down Fore Street. Here, fires are blazing on both sides of the road; burnt-out and abandoned fire appliances lie smouldering in the roadway, their rubber tyres completely melted. The rubble from collapsed buildings lying three and four feet deep makes progress difficult in the extreme. Scrambling and jumping, we use the bigger bits of masonry as stepping-stones, and eventually reach the outskirts of the stricken area.[5]

The popular American journalist Ernie Pyle was in London during the Blitz. At the height of the bombing that night, he went out onto the balcony of his room:

> You have all seen big fires, but I doubt if you have ever seen the whole horizon of a city lined with great fires – scores of them, perhaps hundreds. There was something inspiring just in the awful savagery of it. The closest fires were near enough for us to hear the crackling flames and the yells of firemen. Little fires grew into big ones even as we watched. Big ones died down under the firemen's valor, only to break out again later. About every two minutes a new wave of planes would be over. The motors seemed to grind rather than roar, and to have an angry pulsation, like a bee buzzing in blind fury… Into the dark shadowed spaces below us, while we watched, whole batches of incendiary bombs fell. We saw two dozen go off in two seconds. They flashed terrifically, then quickly simmered down to pin points of dazzling white, burning ferociously. These white pin

5. See www.alondoninheritance.com.

points would go out one by one, as the unseen heroes of the moment smothered them with sand. But also, while we watched, other pin points would burn on, and soon a yellow flame would leap up from the white center. They had done their work – another building was on fire.[6]

A City Ablaze

Most Londoners, such as journalist Peter Ritchie Calder, who became Director of Plans and Campaigns at the Political Warfare Executive, could do nothing but watch helplessly, as the bombs fell and the buildings burned:

Flames licked round the walls as though they were sampling a fresh tit-bit; then thrust through the windows and attacked the stores hungrily. Beams caught alight. The roofs slowly sagged as though they were gelatine, and then crashed with a roar. A container would explode and add fresh fuel to the flames. Floors would be eaten through and collapse in succession and then, with each new gift of stores, the fires would leap up.[7]

Listening to the radio in her flat in Cholmley Gardens, Hampstead, thankfully some 5 miles from the worst of the fires, Gwladys Cox was awake throughout the Luftwaffe's assault. A knock on her door heralded the arrival of an excited neighbour who urged Gwladys to head upstairs to see the scene that was developing across the city.

Gwladys later noted in her diary:

So went upstairs, and, from their top floor window, facing south-east, with its wide, uninterrupted view of London away to the East End, we watched… a spectacle of the most terrible beauty I have ever witnessed. It was a dark and moonless night and the whole sky to the east, above the City, was a vivid sheet of flame… we realised at once that the conflagration centred round St. Paul's… volumes of rose-pink smoke and many-coloured flashes from explosions pierced again and again the blood-red clouds which, brooding and angry, hung for miles over the City.[8]

Teenager Frederick Thomson was, along with his family, also at home in his flat as the bombers began their work. Unlike Gwladys, however, he was a little closer to the action, the family residence being on the Ethelred Estate in Kennington. It 'being as light as day' when the 'All Clear' sounded, Frederick headed out to explore the surrounding area: 'What a sight! No longer the roar of bombers or the crunch of bombs, just the crackle of flames… A warehouse adjacent to the Etheld [sic] Estate where we lived was engulfed in flames. One floor after another collapsed until the building was a burned-out shell. All the time what I believe was tins of paint were going 'bang' and jumping in the air.'[9]

Jumping on his bicycle, Frederick headed off north towards Southwark Street. 'That was enough', he declared. 'There were fire hoses all over the road and although the firemen were having a real "go", I watched one building after another crash to the ground. That raid of fire created the biggest area of devastation in Britain, about one square mile north of St. Paul's Cathedral, including the Barbican district.'

Though the raid ended at 21.45 hours, the fires burned through the night and into the following morning. Such was the extent of the destruction, an American journalist telegraphed his office describing what he called the 'Second Great Fire of London'. In fact, the damage was even more severe than that that had started in Thomas Farriner's bakery in Pudding Lane in 1666.

Just a few hundred yards to the north of Pudding Lane, senior clerk B J Rogers went up to the roof of the Bank of England with other bank officials: 'Here an appalling sight met our eyes. The whole of London seemed alight. We were hemmed in by a wall of flame in every direction. It was not just big fires just here and there, but a continuous sheet of flame all around. And so close! … Altogether a wonderful and terrifying sight.'[10]

---

6. Ernie Pyle, *Ernie Pyle in England* (Robert M. McBride, New York, 1945).
7. Quoted in Gaskin, op cit, p.24.
8. Quoted in David Johnson, op cit, p.158.
9. Frank and Joan Shaw, *We Remember the Blitz* (Ebury Press, London, 2012), p.332.
10. Quoted in Gaskin, op cit, pp.259–60.

Above: One of many AFS personnel recognised for the actions and gallantry during the Blitz, Section Officer M Pennington of Southwark Fire Station shows her OBE to fellow AFS personnel following her investiture in March 1941. (Historic Military Press)

Left: Firemen examine some of their vehicles that were burnt out by the raging fires on 29 December. In use at the time, they had to be abandoned when the flames, unable to be held back by the firemen, enveloped them. (Historic Military Press)

Above left: The fire- and bomb-damaged interior of London's Guildhall after the attack on 29 December. (Historic Military Press)

Above right: A victim of a later raid, St George's Cathedral was hit by an incendiary bomb on the night of 16 April 1941. As this picture of its empty shell reveals, the subsequent fire consumed the wooden roof and much else. (Historic Military Press)

Though earlier raids had seen more enemy aircraft over London delivering more bombs and incendiaries than on 29 December, and others had lasted far longer, none caused as much damage, because of the nature of the targets and the timing of the attack. The Square Mile contained 31 guild halls and 19 churches (including eight built by Sir Christopher Wren), which were all razed to the ground. Paternoster Row, in London's publishing district, was also decimated, with some 20 publishing houses wrecked or badly damaged. About five million books were destroyed in the fires. So much had been lost to the flames that just a few hours later across the Atlantic, the *New York Times* declared: 'Old London is irreplaceable'.

Members of the Pioneer Corps, employed on clearance work in London during early 1941, are pictured taking a break in a bomb-damaged theatre. (Historic Military Press)

Chapter 15

Blitz Crime

With the fall of night came the terrifying wail of the sirens, the deep rumble of aircraft and the stunning detonation of the bombs. Into the shelters rushed the families and the shop keepers, the maids and the landlords. Out into the streets went the wardens, the firemen, the police, the soldiers and the criminals. For the latter, the Blitz would present an opportunity for rich pickings.

Between 1939 and 1945, reported crimes in England and Wales rose from 303,711 to 478,394, an increase of 57 per cent. 'The blackout and the bombs were the most obvious factors', notes the author Mark Ellis, but 'murder, rape, robbery, burglary and theft all flourished in the dark and the chaos'.[1]

A Looter's Paradise

Among the crimes that the war suddenly created, or made more prevalent, was looting. It was certainly a common offence during the Blitz. Looting is, writes Roy Ingleton, 'a repellent word – it conjures up images of human ghouls moving surreptitiously among the dead and dying in the hope of picking up some unguarded valuables'.[2] In reality, looting was a straightforward case of theft aggravated by the circumstances of the war. So serious did the authorities take the threat of such crimes, that, under Defence Regulation 38A, the death penalty could be applied to those found guilty of such acts in war-damaged areas.

The social historian Juliet Gardiner agrees that 'looting can be a rather elastic term'. She adds that:

There are stories about rescue parties going to a pub and having to dig for bodies, which is a very grisly task; one of the leaders of such a rescue party found a bottle of brandy and passed it round his men to have a swig to stiffen their sinews and he was actually sentenced to six months in prison. It was mitigated on appeal, but it gives you an idea of what a broad spectrum the notion of looting could cover.[3]

The view taken by many people was that 'although "looting" was heavily punished, often it involved no more than finding a use for scare articles being ruined by the weather'.[4] Any object, it seems, was considered fair game for looting by ordinary, usually law-abiding people, who would never, under normal peace-time conditions, have ever thought of stealing. The Commissioner of Police observed in 1941 that looting 'is an offence varying widely in magnitude and in the class of person by whom it is committed'.

Though it was reported in debate in the House of Commons on 26 June 1941, that in the preceding 12 months there had been '4,584 cases of looting in London alone', it was far from a problem confined just to the capital. In Dover, for example, the Chief Inspector of the local CID reported that whole rows of houses had been ransacked by looters. 'In cases where there are several houses bombed out in one street, the looters have systematically gone through the lot', reported Percy Datlen. 'Carpets have been stripped from the floors, stair carpets have been removed: they have even taken away heavy mangles, bedsteads and complete suites of furniture.'[5]

For children, the bombed houses and shops were Aladdin's caves. One man, Brian Saville, recalled his childhood in the war, with fond memories of when his local sweetshop was hit by a bomb. His and his brother's weekly pocket money would never stretch to the luxury of chocolate, and they craved for one product in particular that sat on the top shelf in the sweetshop – Walnut Whips. On one night in November, a landmine

---

1. Mark Ellis, '10 Facts About Crime on the Home Front', www.historyextra.com.
2. Roy Ingleton, *The Gentlemen at War – Policing Britain 1939–45* (Maidstone, 1994), p.265.
3. Mark Ellis, op cit.
4. Norman Longmate, *The Home Front* (Chatto & Windus, London, 1984), p.99.
5. Donald Thomas, *An Underworld at War: Spivs, Deserters, Racketeers & Civilians in the Second World War* (John Murray, London, 2003), pp.77–8.

fell in the centre of the local parade of shops. The next morning, Brian and his brother went out to see what damage had been done to his neighbourhood. 'I wandered around outside looking at the devastation', Brian has since written. 'Just around the corner we found the contents of the sweetshop on the pavement and in the gutter. The coveted Walnut Whips were there for all to see, and we unashamedly filled our pockets.'

In August 1940, a man took a few tablets of soap from a bomb-damaged factory in Croydon. He was vilified by the newspapers as 'The Air Raid Looter'. In September 1940, a defendant was told by a magistrate that he had committed 'a capital offence' by stealing two shoes from a bomb-damaged shop, whilst, in January 1941, a man and two women were caught searching for coal in the debris of the ruins of St Mark's Church in Holloway. They were charged with looting – the coal in their sacks was valued at two shillings.

Often, some of the main targets were coin-in-the-slot electricity meters – a source of ready cash. After heavy bombing raids upon Coventry in 1940, it is said that people 'poured' into the city to look at the devastation and to see what they could steal. As many as a quarter of all the meters removed from bomb-damaged houses in Coventry were found to have been broken open.[6]

It was not only the public who were found to have been looting. One source states that no less than 42 per cent of proven cases of looting were committed by people in official positions, or members of the civil defence organisations.[7] A War Reserve Constable called Frank Whipple told of his experiences around the docks in London: 'There was a terrible lot of looting. You'd find bent wardens, heavy rescue men, even police doing it. People were like vultures, going into bombed-out houses and shops.'

One author noted that:

There was widespread pocketing of valuables from bombed houses by demolition squads and even by auxiliary firemen or rescue workers. A blind eye was turned: it was often regarded as a reward for their gruesome task. 'Our sergeant says loot as much as you like as long as you're not found out', claimed one auxiliary fireman… A girl in the AFS was said to bring home something every night, but often it was nothing more valuable than a tin of pineapples.

Of 50 cases heard at the Old Bailey on 9 November 1940, 20 involved looting, of which ten concerned members of the AFS. Three months later, 32 men of the Royal Engineers were brought before the same court for removing lead from bombed houses and passing it on to a local scrap metal merchant. The soldiers even used army lorries and drivers to transport the recovered metal.

Instances of looting became so widespread that at the Leeds Assizes on 5 March 1941, the judge, Justice of the Peace Charles, complained that more than two whole days of court time had been taken in dealing with cases of looting that had occurred in just one city – Sheffield – alone.

There were rich pickings to be had, and as a result, the casual opportunist was soon joined in looting by organised criminals. 'It was claimed that, in London, gangs of looters employed "spotters" to identify likely properties for looting', noted Roy Ingleton. 'The owners of the shops and factories would return to their shattered premises to find them completely striped of all valuables and stock.'

After the Blitz, the regional manager of the Cardiff office of the War Damage Commission wrote a damming report on the subject of looting:

The evil is at its height immediately after a blitz, but it continues until there is little left that is worth removing. Even fruit trees in gardens are uprooted and stolen. Baths, fireplaces, copper tanks, whole staircases, etc are removed undamaged, which demand a certain amount of skill. It is evident that the looting (as distinct from wilful damage) is not the work of irresponsible youths. How the culprits succeed in carting the articles away without being detected is a mystery to me.[8]

---

6. Norman Longmate, *Air Raid – The Bombing of Coventry, 1940* (Arrow, London, 1976), p.243.
7. Edward Smithies, *Crime in Wartime – A Social History of Crime in World War II* (Allen & Unwin, London, 1982), p.49.
8. Todd Gray, *Looting in Wartime Britain* (Mint Press, Exeter, 2009), p.67.

Above: A cordon blocks off a street in the City of London due to an unexploded bomb – an ideal situation for criminals to perpetrate their acts. (Historic Military Press)

Left: Police officers evacuating residents after a 2,500lb unexploded bomb was reported opposite University College Hospital, London, during the Blitz in 1941. Such individuals might well return to their homes to discover they had been the victims of theft. (Library of Congress)

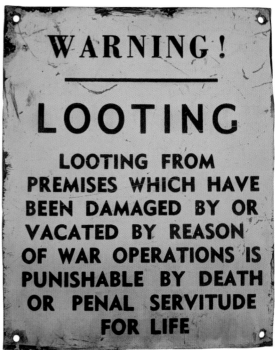

Above left: A Civil Defence worker sets the time for the start of the blackout on a house in London during the Blitz. (Historic Military Press)

Above right: A wartime enamel sign warning of the punishments that a looter might receive. (Courtesy of Terry Parsons)

Shattered shops in London's Oxford Street at the height of the Blitz. In 1940, there were 426 cases of theft (looting) dealt with under the Defence Regulations as opposed to the peacetime legislation; in 1941, this figure was 508. (Historic Military Press)

The 'Blackout Ripper'

In his report for 1943, the Commissioner of the Metropolitan Police, Sir Philip Game, concluded that the bulk of crime in Britain consisted of 'burglary, house and shop breakings and stealing of all kind'. That said, with cities plunged into darkness by the blackout, and normal routines disrupted, other more pernicious forms of crime, such as muggings, rape and even murder, continued to occur. Convictions for both manslaughter and murder averaged at around 99 per annum during the war period, rising 'only a little' from the pre-war years, peaking at 122 in 1945 – though this is thought to have been a consequence of servicemen returning from overseas.

One individual who took full advantage of conditions imposed by the war was Harry Dobkin. Dobkin murdered his wife in April 1941 and buried her under the debris of bomb-blasted Vauxhall Baptist Chapel, hoping she would be discovered as an air raid victim. Her body was not found for more than a year – at which point the police pathologist revealed that strangulation had been the cause of death. Found guilty at his trial, Dobkin was executed at Wandsworth Prison in January 1943.

Even more harrowing is the story surrounding 28-year-old Leading Aircraftman Gordon Frederick Cummins, albeit it is one that began after the Blitz proper had ended. Under the cover of darkness, Cummins stalked the bomb-ravaged streets and pubs of Whitechapel, Marylebone and the West End in search of his victims.

On Monday, 9 February 1942, the body of Evelyn Hamilton was found in a surface air-raid shelter on Montagu Place in Marylebone. She had been strangled. Within hours, another body was discovered by two meter readers for the Central London Electricity Company in a flat on Wardour Street. Evelyn Oakley had also been murdered in a particularly gruesome manner.

Margaret Lowe was victim number three, strangled with her own stockings in the second week of February. That the killer was still on the loose became clear on 12 February, with the discovery of the body of Doris Jouannet.

At this point, the press latched on to the fact that a possible serial killer was at large – an individual they soon dubbed the 'Blackout Ripper'. Whilst attacking a fifth victim, Cummins was challenged by a night porter and ran off. He left behind his respirator that carried his service number. This was one of the clues that led the police to Cummins, who was promptly arrested.

His trial opened at the Old Bailey on 27 April 1942. The proceedings lasted just one and a half days. Cummins, who had already been dishonourably discharged from the RAF, took the stand using the defence that he was too drunk on each of the stated occasions to remember anything. The 12-man jury retired at 16.00 hours on the 28th. They returned just 35 minutes later; found guilty, Cummins was sentenced to death by hanging.

Cummins never admitted his crimes nor explained the reasons for his murder spree. This left the police with an unsolved puzzle. Four months before Cummins' savage rampage, a girl's partially clothed body was found in a bombed-out house in Soho. Maple Church was found beaten and strangled, and she had wounds on her arms and legs. Had she actually been the 'Blackout Ripper's' first victim?

Above left: **Buildings in London, having been bombed and virtually destroyed in a Luftwaffe raid on 1 December 1940, with the owners' possessions on show and open to the elements. (Historic Military Press)**

Above right: **A row of bombed houses in London pictured on 3 November 1940. Note the piles of residents' possessions left out in the street. (Historic Military Press)**

Chapter 16

The Deadliest Night

They had survived. For eight months, the people of London had survived the longest aerial bombardment the world had known, and, though it seemed that the attacks would go on forever, they had adapted to what had become a new normal. Indeed, it seemed that rather than the bombs of the Luftwaffe grinding down Londoners, it was the Luftwaffe that was flagging, its efforts declining, its crews tiring and its losses mounting as the fighter pilots of the RAF grew stronger and more efficient.

On the ground also, the emergency and civil services had become welded into an effective force, capable of dealing with anything the enemy threw at it. Techniques had improved in the recovery of those trapped under buildings, in maintaining communications when telephone lines had been cut, in directing first aiders to the injured and in maintaining order and controlling fires.

With the longer days of the spring of 1941, the operations of the enemy aircraft were also becoming increasingly confined to the diminishing hours of darkness. No longer was there a need to scurry home after a difficult day's work, there was time to join the crowds at the pubs and the clubs where the worries of the war were drunk and danced away. As one Australian living in London remarked of the capital's citizens: 'Nothing in the air, on the earth and on the water scares them. They get annoyed but they never get scared.' But as midnight approached on 10 May 1941, so did the enemy. The hours of darkness ahead would become London's deadliest of the war.

It was to be the last great raid of the Blitz before Hitler launched his invasion of the Soviet Union, for which increasing numbers of aircraft would be drawn away to the East. Every effort was to be made by the Luftwaffe, with some crews undertaking two or three sorties in the night. Whilst their main targets were the bridges west of Tower Bridge, factories on the south side of the Thames, the warehouses at Stepney and the railway line that ran north from Elephant and Castle, in reality, much of the capital suffered severely.

Announcing the imminent arrival of the German bombers, the sirens had first begun their 'awful warbling-like sound of a howling wolf', as one London resident, Joan Veazey, described in her diary, at 22.53 hours in Croydon. In Westminster, it was exactly 23.00 hours, and in Kennington, it was two minutes past the hour.

Leading the Luftwaffe's aerial armada were 21 Heinkel He 111s of Hauptmann Kurd Aschenbrenner's Kampfgruppe 100. As before, their task was to light up the target for the bombers of Kampfgruppe 54 and Kampfgruppe 55, which were following behind. The crews of Kampfgruppe 100 released their incendiary bombs just as the Westminster sirens had begun to wail.

Blackout restrictions had been eased only the day before by the Metropolitan Police and public houses could stay open until 22.00 hours, giving their customers 20 minutes to reach home before the curtains had to be drawn and lights hidden from the bomb-aimers above. At 23.02 hours, the first of the incendiaries began to fall through the cloudless moonlit sky.

'It was a beautiful night, and I was up on Coventry Street', recalled Special Constable Ballard Berkeley, who was on his beat in the West End. 'When I was on duty, the sirens had gone and the City was being bombed. The city was getting well lit up. We knew the pattern – the incendiaries would light up the target and then the bombers would come in and bomb.'

This time, the Luftwaffe had arrived in strength. Throughout the course of the night, the Germans would fly 541 sorties against the British capital, with many aircraft returning a second or even third time. Constable Berkeley, who went on to play Major Gowan in the BBC TV comedy classic *Fawlty Towers*, noticed how the Londoners appeared unmoved by the incendiaries. It was the day of the FA Cup Final, and newspaper vendors continued to call out for passers-by to read about the match, whilst others, rather than rushing for the shelters, headed for the Lyons Corner House. They, had, after all, seen this many times before. That night, though, it would be different, very different. It would be the worst night they had experienced.

Above: Firemen play their hoses on dying embers in buildings along Queen Victoria Street on the morning of 11 May 1941. (Historic Military Press)

Left: Another image showing firefighters battling the flames in Queen Victoria Street during the raid on the night of 10/11 May 1941. The international headquarters of the Salvation Army is on the right. (Historic Military Press)

Above: As the original caption states, this is 'a scene of devastation in the City of London after the great fire Blitz of May 1941'. The church is St Giles-without-Cripplegate. (Historic Military Press)

Right: The hole in the roof of Westminster Abbey after it was hit during the night of 10/11 May. (Historic Military Press)

'Suddenly, it happened', explained Constable Berkeley who was deep in the heart of Soho:

I'd heard bombs, been near bombs – but when a bomb hits so close, you don't hear it. It was the most extraordinary thing. Everything stopped and there was complete and utter silence. It was so quiet, it was unbelievable. Perhaps the explosion had deafened the eardrums. I don't know but everything was silent. Nobody moved... After a few seconds, everything came to life – except the people who were dead... I couldn't move. I was standing up, but I couldn't move. I thought my legs had gone but in fact, I was up to my knees in rubble and bricks. That's why I couldn't move.[1]

---

1. Joshua Levine, *Forgotten Voices of the Blitz and the Battle for Britain* (Edbury Press, London, 2007), pp.453–5.

Above left: Bomb damage that can still be seen on the walls of St Clement Danes on the Strand. (Courtesy of Robert Mitchell)

Above right: A photograph showing the damage caused when a bomb tore a hole in the face of Big Ben during the bombing on 10/11 May. (Historic Military Press)

Left: The Old Bailey, scarred by German bombs during the last major raid of the Blitz on London. (Historic Military Press)

A Towering Pillar of Dust

Having been a witness to the start of the Blitz, the American military attaché, General Raymond E Lee, was still in London, staying at the Claridge's Hotel, for this last assault. He recalled:

It did not take long for a few bombs to crack down close to the hotel, shaking it from top to bottom, and when I went to the balcony I could hear them [the German bombers] quite near, apparently overhead... It was dark enough, but the whole sky was lit up by a huge yellowish disc of full moon, while the horizon was illuminated by a great number of fires which extended all around us in a huge ring. As a rule, the fires before had appeared like rose red illuminations, but tonight a large number of them had huge, forked flames leaping up towards the heavens, which indicated to me they were buildings which had been ignited on top by incendiary bombs. I could count not less than fifteen of them all around us, and it really looked as if Claridge's hotel was the exact hub and centre of the whole design. One of the two wardens, who was keeping his post up there, said he was rather hopeful that two or three bombers had been brought down over London because he had seen them come in a steep dive and apparently in flames.

As we were talking to him, there was the usual drone of the falling bomb, and then over towards Piccadilly there was a huge explosion and a towering pillar of dust, debris, smoke and sparks, which shot up like

magic to the zenith. I heard a sudden convulsive movement, and looking round, found that both [Vincent] Sheeran [an American author] and his wife were grovelling flat on the tin roof, which seemed to me rather shocking, because for a moment I felt that a shell fragment or something had stricken them down. After a little while they got up and dusted themselves off. They hardly seemed to realize that after a bomb had gone off there is not much use falling down.[2]

From the offices of the *Daily Mirror*, in Fetters Lane off Fleet Street, the newspaper's chairman, Cecil King, looked across the city:

The smoke was such that you could not see that it was a full moon with no clouds, the air was full of flying sparks; every now and then there was a roar of a collapsing building... The Temple Church, one of the great monuments of English history, was on fire... St Clement Dane had been gutted, and only the spire was alight halfway up the top and sending out showers and sparks – an odd and rather beautiful spectacle.[3]

A view of the interior of St Mary-le-Bow in Cheapside after the church was bombed on 10 May 1941. During the subsequent fire, the church's bells crashed to the ground. (Historic Military Press)

2. James Leutze, *The London Observer: The Journal of General Raymond E. Lee 1940-1941* (Hutchinson, London, 1972), pp.270–1.
3. Juliet Gardiner, *The Blitz: The British Under Attack* (Harper Press, London, 2011) p.345.

Above: Another of London's churches that was hit on the night of 10/11 May 1941, in this case St Olave's Church on Hart Street in the City of London. (Historic Military Press)

Right: The Commons Chamber at the Palace of Westminster was entirely destroyed by the fires that raged after the bombing of 10/11 May 1941. (Historic Military Press)

The Fires Rage

By 23.25 hours, 20 minutes after the first incendiaries had landed, what looked like a dangerous fire situation was already starting to develop in the drab grey streets in and around West Ham. First it was the Royal Albert Docks; next the railway sheds and sidings at the King George V Dock; then a major fire at Mitchell and Snow's, the cork merchants. On the roof of The Lion public house in West Ham, landlord Bill Barker saw the 'great orange wall of flame as a timber dump took fire across the Temple Mills Sidings'.

As he watched, 'a water tower poked up against the blaze like a steel finger, the firemen at the top clinging grimly to the jet. Suddenly a German plane zoomed low from the clouds; machine-gun fire cracked sharply. The firemen didn't even deign to look around, and presently, as if abashed, the plane went away.'[4]

At West Ham, Fire Chief Herbert Johnson could see that he did not have enough engines to cope with fires that were springing up everywhere and pleaded to Commander Firebrace for help – he asked for 20 engines to stand by.

But the fires were soon raging across the city, and fire engines and firefighters were needed everywhere. At her home in Maida Vale, Olive Jones was in bed trying to get to sleep when there was a 'tremendous loud howling whistle from a falling fire bomb' that had landed in the garden of the house next door. 'I ran out, shouting to the maids, and with some difficulty pulled myself over the wall by means of a branch of an elder tree at the bottom of the garden and ran to deal with it bareheaded, fully expecting that one of the maids would come in a moment or two.'

---

4. Richard Collier, *The City That Would Not Die, the Bombing of London May 10-11 1941* (E. P. Dutton, New York, 1959), pp.76–7.

No one came to help her. So, using her bare hands, she covered the incendiary with soil and then found a bucket with enough water in it to extinguish the device. Just as she had put out the incendiary, a high explosive bomb fell. She later wrote in her diary:

A tremendous outburst of noise thundered from the sky, I ran like a hare to the wall... I scraped myself over the wall somehow in a flap because of the noise as if the heavens were falling, but only to find myself... inextricably entangled in the tree branches. I was still half-blinded by the brightness of the fire bomb and the awful blitz noise that filled the air... for what seemed like hours I dithered and fumbled on the wall top, clawing frantically at the twigs that encircled me and caught in my clothes.

Eventually, Olive fought herself free – and expressed her displeasure in no uncertain terms to the 'blithering and giggling' maids.[5]

A Memorable Souvenir

At Waterloo, two vital water mains had been damaged by bombs, and the area was virtually devoid of water to tackle the fires. To make the situation even more critical, the bombing was, as had been the case on 29 December, taking place at the ebb of a spring tide, and the water level in the Thames was frustratingly low.

The bombing was not confined to any particular part of London, and bombs fell even on its northern limits at Barnett, where the family of Geoff Stanfield, then aged nine, lived:

We were bombed at around 11pm. Four bombs in all; one three houses along from us, one on the allotment at the bottom of the garden and two further away. The various blasts blew the curtains in and most of the

Employees of Selfridge's department store examine damage done to the shop's Palm Court on the night of 10/11 May. (Historic Military Press)

5. Gavin Mortimer, *The Longest Night, 10-11 May 1941, Voices from the London Blitz* (Cassell, London, 2011), pp.154–5.

A building collapses, adding to the rubble already lying in the roadway on Ludgate Hill, near St Paul's Cathedral, after the attack on 10/11 May 1941. (Historic Military Press)

windows out, some ceilings out and plaster came in. My sister and I, who were sleeping in a double bed in a downstairs rear room, were still asleep beneath curtains, dust and plaster etc. Dad had been in the kitchen making cocoa, and finished up amidst all the pots and pans. Mum had been standing in the doorway to our room and was narrowly missed by the front door, which was blown in. I can still smell the cordite, explosions, plaster, dust and fractured sewers etc. We were dragged out of the house and up the front garden path, and I can remember stooping to pick up a large bomb splinter that had become embedded in the garden gate, now hanging by one hinge: I was promptly pulled away as it was still very hot, but what a souvenir to have had![6]

Bomb blasts can have unpredictable and differing effects, as experienced by two people that night. Home Guard volunteer Ron Mitchell was on guard duty at the docks:

Hearing one loud 'whistle' – I shall never forget the sound of bombs 'whistling' – that seemed headed directly at us – my partner and I dived under a big truck, parked nearby and already loaded with a ton or two of material. We lay flat just under the bonnet of the engine. The bomb actually missed us by a hundred or more yards but we both clearly saw fires all around, plenty of light by which to see the blast lift the wheels of the truck clear of the ground – and drop them within a foot of our heads – that is when we learned that under a truck is NOT a good place to take cover when a bomb falls nearby.[7]

Doug Bowerman was in bed at a block of council flats at 60 Halton Road, Islington, and he too, like the truck that nearly landed on Ron Mitchell, found himself flying through the air:

About midnight during the noise of A.A. fire and bombs falling, I heard the biggest bang I have ever heard in my life. Blast does funny things and in this case I was sucked out of bed, along the hall passage and finished up against the wall of the living/dining room, or where it had been. I have to tell you that Halton Mansions were blocks of 36 flats with two sets of entrances for 16 flats each. I stood up, looked out, and where the other half of the building had been, was a pile of rubble.[8]

The Deadliest Night

The last bomb to fall was timed at 05.37 hours on the morning of the 11th – the 'All Clear' sounded a short while later at 05.50 hours. It landed on Scotland Yard. The 2,932 high explosive bombs, 72 oil-bombs and

---

6. Quoted from www.ww2today.com/10th-may-1941.
7. BBC People's War website, Article A6655430.
8. BBC People's War website, Article A3758141.

77 parachute mines, along with untold numbers of incendiaries, had caused the death of 1,436 Londoners; a further 1,800 people were seriously injured across London. More than 12,000 were left homeless. Fourteen German aircraft were shot down.

The bombs and incendiaries started in excess of 2,000 separate fires, nine of which were classified as 'conflagrations' and 20 as 'major'. Together, these fires consumed an area of about 700 acres of central London and 959 roads were blocked with rubble from collapsed buildings or rendered impassable by huge craters. More than 5,000 houses were destroyed, with a similar number of buildings being severely damaged. A number of iconic London landmarks, such as the Palace of Westminster, Waterloo Station, Westminster Abbey, the British Museum, the Law Courts, Lambeth Palace and St Clement Danes were also hit, in what one historian later referred to as 'the Luftwaffe's last fling' in the Blitz.

Above left: A 'then and now' view of a damaged window and façade near St Stephen's Entrance at the Palace of Westminster. (Comparison by Robert Mitchell)

Above middle: The badly damaged No Lobby in the House of Commons in the immediate aftermath of the bombing. The No Lobby is the room on the left of the Speaker, behind the Opposition benches. (Historic Military Press)

Above right: A 'then and now' image showing bomb fragment damage, caused on the night of 10/11 May, to one of the walls in the Old Palace Yard at the Palace of Westminster. (Comparison by Robert Mitchell)

Chapter 17

'An Unconquerable People'

Though they did not know it on the morning of Sunday, 11 May 1941, the events of the previous few hours would mark the last serious sustained attack that Londoners, and indeed much of the country, would suffer until the V-weapons campaign of 1944.

The following day, the recovery began. Undeterred, people set off for work, somehow finding their way through the tangled ruins to their businesses and offices. One of those was Olive Jones, who drove to the City:

Inching along in clouds of dust and petrol fumes… but everybody… accepted the never-ending wearisomeness of mile-long traffic jams with the most wonderful good humour… [the] most amazing sight was the pedestrians who thronged the thoroughfare. I should hardly thought there were so many people in the world as there seemed to be office workers walking the streets carrying briefcases and type-writers and attaché cases.

As Winston Churchill predicted in June 1940, when the attack upon the United Kingdom was about to begin, Hitler 'knows that he will have to break us in this island or lose the war'. Hitler had tried firstly to defeat the RAF and, when that effort failed, had attempted to break the resolve of the British people with a bombing campaign that had lasted for a staggering eight months and five days.

During those months, and the lesser raids up to the end of 1941, approximately 190,000 bombs were dropped on the UK; 43,667 civilians were killed – 20,178 men, 17,226 women and 5,460 children. The seriously injured numbered 50,387 – 4,016 of whom were children.

The attacks had affected almost every major city in the country, including the industrial heartlands, the coastal towns, the ports and the naval bases. 'I see the damage done by the enemy attacks', Churchill told the nation on 12 April 1941, 'but I also see side by side with the devastation and amid the ruins, quiet, confident, bright and smiling eyes, beaming with a consciousness of being associated with a cause far higher and wider than any human or personal issue. I see the spirit of an unconquerable people.'

Just how much the towns and cities of Britain had suffered during the Blitz is vividly illustrated by this view of part of the procession of the Lord Mayor's Show making its way through the Blitzed streets of London, in this case Cannon Street on the way to the Law Courts, on 9 November 1945. (Historic Military Press)

Despite the Prime Minister's optimism, the Luftwaffe was far from done with its campaigns against the British population. In late April 1942, for example, it launched a series of raids that came to be known as the 'Baedeker Blitz'.

The previous month, Bomber Command had carried out a devastating attack on the Hanseatic port of Lübeck, destroying much of the old, timber-built city in a test of the Allies' new 'area bombing' strategy. An enraged Hitler ordered that the Luftwaffe immediately respond. The similarly historic British cities that were duly targeted were selected, it is said, by reason of their 'three-star' status in the famous pre-war Baedeker travel guides. Exeter, Bath, Norwich, Canterbury and York were among the various destinations that the German bomber crews paid a visit to.

Even as the Battle of Britain had been drawing to a close, the Luftwaffe began arming its single-engine fighters with bombs, using them in preference to twin-engine bombers against daylight targets. Often little more than nuisance raids, except of course when a bomb exploded in your immediate vicinity, these so-called 'Tip and Run' attacks continued throughout 1941, before gaining importance in the spring of 1942. Two units were designated for these missions – 10/JG 2 and 10/JG 26 – with the targets extended to include railways, gas holders and selected military and civilian installations. Locations such as Yeovil, Salisbury, the Isle of Wight, Great Yarmouth, Worthing, Torquay and Bournemouth, as well as London, all suffered.

The last strategic air offensive undertaken against the UK by the Luftwaffe's bombers was launched in January 1944. Also known as the 'Baby Blitz', Operation *Steinbock* began on the night of 21/22 January 1944. It commenced with two attacks on London, with about eight hours between each. In total, the two waves involved 447 sorties by aircraft that included the four-engine Heinkel He 177.

Though *Steinbock* was chiefly concerned with attacking the Greater London area, Bristol, Hull, Portsmouth, Plymouth, Weymouth, Falmouth and Torquay were among the conurbations that received the Luftwaffe's attention. Although the attacks had involved more enemy aircraft than any other raids on the UK since 1941, the effectiveness of the Allied air and ground defences, the relative inexperience of the German bomber crews, and the sheer lack of bomber numbers, meant that the Baby Blitz proved to be relatively ineffectual. Already faltering by the end of April 1944, *Steinbock* was abandoned in May.

The reality was that Britain, as a whole, was never broken by Göring's bombers – though few would doubt the severity of their effects or how great the pressure on the public will had at times been. Their incendiaries, high explosive bombs and parachute mines had wrecked buildings and wrecked lives but had not destroyed the British people's overall determination to resist. As a result, Churchill would eventually be proven correct – Hitler would indeed lose the war.

A national symbol of defiance, St Paul's Cathedral survived the German bombing and was naturally selected to mark the last day of World War Two – VJ Day – when it was floodlit as part of the celebrations to mark the end of the fighting. (Historic Military Press)

Other books you might like:

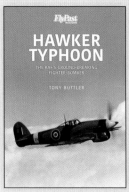

Historic Military Aircraft Series, Vol. 5

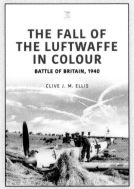

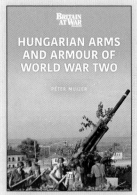

Modern Wars Series, Vol. 3

Military Vehicles and Artillery Series, Vol. 1

For our full range of titles please visit:
shop.keypublishing.com/books

VIP Book Club
Sign up today and receive
TWO FREE E-BOOKS

Be the first to find out about our forthcoming book releases and receive exclusive offers.

Register now at keypublishing.com/vip-book-club

Our VIP Book Club is a 100% spam-free zone, and we will never share your email with anyone else.
You can read our full privacy policy at: privacy.keypublishing.com